THE WINNING POWER
OF PRESSURE DEFENSE
IN BASKETBALL

THE WINNING POWER
OF PRESSURE DEFENSE
IN BASKETBALL

Burrall Paye

PARKER PUBLISHING COMPANY, INC.   West Nyack, N.Y.

© 1974 by
Parker Publishing Company, Inc.

West Nyack, N.Y.

Library of Congress Cataloging in Publication Data

Paye, Burrall,
   The winning power of pressure defense in basketball.

   1. Basketball--Defense. 2. Basketball coaching.
I. Title.
GV888.P39   796.32'32   74-11136
ISBN 0-13-961300-5

Printed In the United States of America

Dedication

I dedicate this book to my associate coach, my wife Nancy, and to a young gentleman who lives and loves the game as much as I do, my son Patrick.

How This Book Will Increase Your Winning Power

It is not uncommon for our ball club to score near the impressive century mark only to find our opponents trailing by forty or fifty points. We have accomplished this at two different small schools with common material. That is defense.

Defense is not only the most consistent phase of basketball; it is the most important. Defensive ball clubs almost never have the bad night. Defense will win the big game.

We have had a life-long love affair with the game of basketball. We attend many clinics each year; we read most of the technical magazines; and we have read over one hundred books devoted solely to the great game of basketball. During all this, there has always seemed to be a neglect on the part of coaches to discuss methods of stopping the offense. Each coach seemed to spend most of his time on the X's and O's of the game. Each coach would consume hours of practice time teaching offensive moves, then teaching a defense without regard to individual defensive moves or techniques.

So basketball literature has been sparse in its coverage of individual pressure defensive methods. The purpose of this book is to help fill that gap. We will introduce such new ideas as front foot to pivot foot pressure stance, team defensive play patterns, and defensive stunting.

The book is written with dual hopes: that it will help develop the coach defensively, and that it will help the player whose offensive ability is limited to make the ball club.

A determined effort has been made to arrange the book in an orderly progression. It begins with an explanation of our individual pressure stances, and evolves into a discussion of our half court pressure team defense and the nine principles that make it work. Following those comments, the book defenses those fundamentals common to all team offenses and enlarges into full court pressure. The when's, why's, and how's are discussed in each chapter.

An added advantage to this book is the drills we use to install our defense. Some of them are unique and different, and while the reader may question their soundness, let me remind him that we are in a unique coaching club, winning at better than 80%, never having had a losing season.

If a coach chooses to use the drills, he will find his offense improving while his defense improves. We use progressive drills, starting with the simple, advancing to the complex. The coach will find as his season progresses that the effectiveness of his ball club improves immeasurably. In fact we hit our peak at tournament time. There has only been one time in our 13 year coaching career that we have not been playing on the final night of the district tournament.

Each chapter is an entity in itself. So if the reader's defense is having trouble at one phase, he should simply turn to the chapter dealing with that malady and cure the illness. For example, Chapter 7 is broken into most of the offensive part plays known to basketball, then defensed: the first four sections deal with individual cuts, the next seven cover the two men game when the ball is involved, the next two areas defense the post cutters, and the last five are involved with team cuts by more than two men. These part plays are the backbone of all team offenses. With this information a defensive coach can subdue the opponents' strengths and exploit their weaknesses.

The most rewarding aspect of this book is its fundamental soundness. Because this basic defense has year-to-year carry over value, the more years it is put into use the more amazed the reader will be at its effectiveness. Using these techniques, players keep improving as they advance in years and the coach never gets caught with that lean rebuilding year.

All the chapters combined will not only give the team a championship defense but they will give the coach a perfect base upon which he can build his own favorite mountain of defenses. But don't build the mountain without this foundation, or one wintry night the coach will find he only had a mole hill.

Burrall Paye

Acknowledgements

I owe.

I owe the greats, the near-greats, and the unknowns who have coached and played this great game. I have gone to many clinics where they have spoken, and I have taken careful notes from them. I have read and borrowed ideas from their published works.

I owe Mr. Herman Masin, Editor of *Scholastic Coach*, for his careful guidance and for his permitting me to use some of my published material from his magazine.

I owe all the players who have played for me, each of whom, in their many individual ways, has contributed greatly to my knowledge of the game.

I owe the many assistant coaches who have served untiringly so that our program could be the success that it is, especially my assistants at Powell Valley: Dave Bently, Eddie Neff, and Donald Pruitt.

To all of them and to the many players who are yet to come, I respectfully submit this book, hoping that in some way it will be a down payment on the basketball debts I owe.

Contents

3 How the Guards Play Defense • 42

4 How to Defense the Corner, the Cutter • 67

5 How to Defense the Inside • 92

6 Methods of Getting Control of the Ball • 122

After A Successful Score
Turnovers

1. Center Jump
2. Held Balls
3. Charging
4. Violations
5. Intercepting Passes
6. Forcing Free Balls and Recovering Them
7. Forcing Bad Shots

Rebounding

1. Reverse Pivots
2. Front Pivots
3. Facing
4. Cross Blockouts
5. Weakside Blockouts
6. Wall or Triangular Rebounding
7. Positioning
8. Securing the Ball
9. Holding Onto the Ball

   a. Little Man
   b. Big Man

7 Breaking Down and Defensing Pattern Basketball • 141

How a Pattern Destroys Offense and Helps Defense
How a Pattern Helps Offense and Hurts Defense
The Complete Pattern Team Can Be Shut Out
Most Coaches Break Their Offense Into Drills
All Team Offenses Have Same Fundamentals

1. Stopping the Give and Go
2. Defensing the Backdoor Cut
3. Defensing the Middle Cut
4. Defensing the Go Behind
5. Defensing the Screen and Roll
6. Defensing the Blind Pick
7. Defensing the Inside Screen
8. Defensing the Dribbling Screen
9. Defensing the Screen and Go Behind
10. Don't Let Them Shoot Over a Screen

THE WINNING POWER
OF PRESSURE DEFENSE
IN BASKETBALL

ONE

Individual Defense: Stance and Movement

Coaches should develop their individual defense before they turn their attention to team defense. The old postulate, "Team defense is only as strong as its weakest link," is very true.

Most coaches spend hours of practice time perfecting the footwork necessary for good offensive play, then neglect the footwork of defensive play. This chapter not only develops good defensive footwork, but it also includes our individual pressure stances.

HOW TO DEVELOP THE TWO BASICS: QUICKNESS AND BODY BALANCE

1. Quickness

What constitutes quickness? A player sights an object, a message is sent to the brain, and a reply comes back to the hands and feet. The faster the relay system, the quicker one is.

Two things speed the report along: concentration and anticipation. Both must be fully developed if the players are to have the desired quickness necessary for playing this defense.

We teach our entire defense by progressive drills. Concentration and anticipation are no exception. They will be developed in almost all of our early team defensive drills.

Quickness is not only a mental skill but also must be developed muscularly. Unfortunately, there are a lot of objects that offer friction, slowing down the defensive man. The first and most important is the friction between shoe and floor.

In our section on stance, we will write of the importance of being on the balls of the feet. Now the defensive man must learn to glide along the floor without letting his feet touch the floor. We know that is impossible, but the closer we get to the impossible, the quicker our feet move.

Drill No. 1 is used to teach this quickness of foot.

Procedure

1. One player with a coach facing him, preferably at a line on the court.
2. The player moves only one step in the direction the coach points.
3. It should be a long step.
4. The player should be in a perfect defensive stance.
5. The coach should always check the stance and perfect it.
6. The coach can alter the drill by using a basketball or movement of his eyes instead of pointing.

Objectives

1. To teach stance.
2. To teach first step movement, the most important step in both offense and defense.
3. To teach concentration and anticipation, prerequisites to quickness.

We purposely set the drill up individually with a coach to examine the athlete closely. It is vital to good defense that quickness, body balance, and stance be superbly developed prior to teaching movement. We spend a considerable amount of early practice time on them because it is easier to teach the correct method than to try to reteach and develop an incorrect one.

We never allow the defender's feet to get more than a fraction of an inch off the floor. Any greater distance would slow down his movement; any less distance would result in unwanted floor-shoe friction. The defensive player must be taught to have this quickness yet to keep his balance. It is as important as teaching the fundamental mechanics of a jump shot.

Drill No. 2 starts with the same basic set-up, a coach and a player. We call it: "Get in Motion Drill." The player is to tap the floor with the balls of his feet as fast as he can. The coach should put his head on the floor, making sure that there is as little daylight as possible between the balls of the feet and the floor on each tap. This drill lasts only about 15 seconds. This is a single purpose drill used only to develop quickness.

Drill No. 3 has the same line up. The coach uses a ball and acts as though he passes in one direction. The player quickly turns and jumps one step toward that direction. This not only teaches quickness, but it is the beginning of our basic defense. Instead of the threat of a pass, the coach may dribble. We use only one dribble to begin, increasing the number of dribbles as the defender improves. In the case of a dribble, the defender pushes off his weakside foot and takes a long step with his strong foot.

The next progressive step in developing our defense is to repeat the same three drills, only adding the arms and hands. As the ball is faked in one direction, our arms and hands fly in that direction. If it is a bounce pass, the hands go down; if it is a chest pass, the arms go out; it it is a lob pass, the arms go up.

The hands must also be taught to be quick; the quicker the better. One of our favorite drills is to line a player up one yard away from the wall, facing it. Give him a partner with a basketball directly behind him. The player with the ball throws it against the wall; the other player tries to retrieve it with one hand before it can hit the floor. This is a dual purpose drill because it teaches ball control while it is teaching reaction by the hand.

Another drill we use has three players, all in a straight line (Drill No. 4). Player C has the ball while player B is facing A. C throws the ball in a bounce, chest, or small lob pass toward player A. At the same time player C yells "now," or the coach can let A give B a visual signal, and player B jumps around, locates the ball, and tries to control it or at least deflect it. This drill is used not only to teach quickness of hand, but also concentration, correct passing techniques, and ball control.

Almost all of our drills are multi-purpose drills in order to save practice time. And almost all of our drills are video command as opposed to audio command because the game of basketball is played by sight, not sound.

2. Body Balance

Without body balance, there is no individual defense, only excessive fouling. Body balance is the foundation upon which good individual defense is built. With body balance, there are infinite possibilities.

The weight of the body must be firmly established directly over both feet. The trunk must be low; and the faster a player is required to be on balance, the lower his center of gravity must be.

Although we teach body balance in several dual purpose drills, we use one initially to develop it (Drill No. 5).

Procedure

1. Place all players in a straight line on one side of the court.
2. Coach gives signal (visual) to let players begin running.
3. Players stop on second signal. They may stop by running stride stop or by a jump stop.
4. Coaches check stop to see if balance was kept.
5. The lower the buttocks at the moment of stop, the better one can maintain balance.
6. When the player's body balance has improved sufficiently, the coach may have the players immediately raise their buttocks to normal guarding position and get into the pat-the-floor drill, readying them for an advance drill.

Objectives

1. To teach body balance.
2. To teach stride and jump stopping.
3. To teach visual concentration.

After commencing the pat the floor drill, we can require one step slides or many steps or some other maneuver which the imagination might conjure. Thus, the reader can see the progressive aspects of this drill as the season advances.

Drill No. 6 is used to develop better body balance as the defensive man retreats.

Procedure

1. Place players at the end of the court in three lines.
2. They are to run sideways or backwards, keeping their eyes on visual command of the coach.
3. The faster they run, the harder it is to control their balance, and the quicker they develop better balance.

Objectives

1. To teach game-like retreating downcourt on defense.
2. To teach body balance while moving at full speed.
3. To condition.
4. To develop quickness in visual reception and communication.

DEFENSIVE FAKES

Fakes are not restricted to offense. They must be used by the defense if it is to dictate and dominate. Fakes are used primarily to disguise the defender's real move, to throw the offense off balance, and to control the opponent.

Fakes must be quick like the strikes of a snake. They must be planned and carried out with precision without losing body balance. The fakes must be deceptive. We have two that have been exceptionally good to us.

The first we call "In and Out." It starts with the same mass drill that we used for body balance (Drill No. 5). When the players gain their balance, we have them work on the pat-the-floor drill; then, on a movement of the basketball we require a half step in toward the ball as the arm and hand on that side strike in. We quickly move back, hardly touching the floor. When facing this in a game situation, the offense will usually hesitate a few moments, then go away from the fake. That is what we want them to do, and it illustrates controlling and dominating the offense.

The second fake we encourage begins when the opponent has his back to us, such as after a rebound off their defensive board or when we have overplayed the offense and they are beginning to run a dribbling reverse. We let them see us take a step in one direction, then we change pace and race hard to the other side. Many times the offense will turn directly into us, charging or walking or committing some violation.

We allow the players to develop any defensive fake of their own. We do not try to limit their defensive effectiveness, but we insist upon the above two fakes.

LIMITING THE OFFENSIVE FAKES THAT CAN BE USED

One-on-one basketball is not championship basketball. Team basketball, on both offense and defense, will win the coveted crown. However, a good basketball player must be able to recognize an individual situation developing, and he must be able to exploit it. Conversely, the defensive player must be able to recognize the developing situation, and he must be prepared to stop it.

The defense has the advantage. He is already three feet closer to the basket. He also knows that regardless of the fakes employed by the offense, the defense can limit the effectiveness to only three moves: one move with the dribble left (drive away from the pivot foot) and two moves once the offense puts the ball on the floor (reverse and crossover dribble).

Our seventh drill is used, among other things, to teach front foot to pivot foot stance.

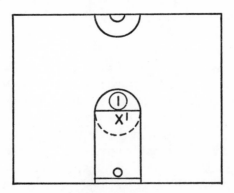

Diagram 1-1

Procedure

1. 1 has the basketball and may use any fake he desires.
2. 1 may not dribble.
3. 1 may shoot whenever he gets X1 off balance but not a forced shot.
4. X1 must use front foot to pivot foot stance.
5. X1 must not leave his feet until 1 has left his.
6. X1 must keep his hand extended, making his reach four inches longer.
7. Coach can stand where X1 does not see him, hold up fingers to allow 1 that many dribbles. We limit it at first to dribbles in only one direction. We start out with no dribbles, then move to one, then two, etc. This makes it progressive and it keeps X1 from cheating.
8. 1 must use right foot as pivot foot one time, then left foot as pivot foot the next.

Objectives

1. To teach our staggered stance, front foot to pivot foot.
2. To teach coverage of man who still has his dribble.
3. To teach good defense of jump shot.
4. To teach offensive moves.
5. To teach shooting under pressure, and when not to shoot.

We are strong advocates of this method of pressure to stop the attacker when he still has his dribble. The teams that use the parallel stance concede the jump shot, the most deadly of the offensive arsenal. That is suicide. The teams that use the front foot to non-pivot foot staggered stance are very vulnerable to the rocker step or any offensive fake toward the advanced foot. In fact, offensive minded coaches teach their players to attack the advance foot of the defense. This is why we advocate front foot to pivot foot staggered stance.

For the sake of defense the coach must determine if the offensive player shoots better on the move or standing still. As a rule, the black players will shoot better on the move, and the white players will shoot better standing still. If the attacker shoots on the move a greater percentage of the time, is he better going to the left or right?

We played against a player who was leading the state in scoring, and we found that his percentage was far less than his average percentage when he shot from a standing still position. We encouraged him to shoot without the dribble; we beat them badly.

Another time we played against an outstanding ball player whose percentage was exceptional when allowed to shoot going toward his left, despite his being right handed. If he went to his right or stood still to shoot, his percentage was much less than his average percentage. Although he averaged over 38 points for the year, we forced him to his right, allowing him only 6 points in both games.

But, on the other hand, we played against a boy who averaged 52% for the year. We charted him on many occasions and found that he hit better than 50% going to his right or left or standing still.

If a team is going to beat all these clubs, it must be able to handle all three types of players. The main objective of the defensive man should be to force the offensive man into the move where the offense will have the least effective percentage of scoring.

The objective of the offense is to get the shot away and to score. The defensive objective should be in the same order; prevent the player from getting the shot away, and then, should the offense succeed in getting the shot off, the defensive man should make him raise the shot, shoot more quickly and thus throw the shot off target. (We introduce Drill No. 8 at this time because it teaches making the offense raise its shot.) Basketball, under the second objective, becomes a game of percentages.

Procedure

1. 1, 2, and 3 have basketballs and are to use pump fakes (we teach three: long; long, short; long, short, short).
2. X1, X2, and X3 are to stay on their feet with extreme pressure until offense goes in air. We would rather have the defenders remain on their feet during

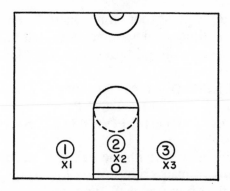

Diagram 1-2

entire drill than to go with a pump fake, allowing an uncontested lay-up.

3. When the offense goes in air, we extend ourselves, not necessarily trying to block the shot.
4. We start with no dribble permitted, but advance to two dribbles, limited at first to only one direction.

Objectives

1. To teach pump faking for use after offensive rebound or after receiving pass in close.
2. To teach defense of the pump fake.
3. To teach extreme pressure when ball is in danger zone.
4. To teach defense on man with ball and dribble left.
5. To teach how to make offense raise the shot.
6. To teach shooting under extreme pressure.

There are only two ways for the offense to score: from a standing still shot (push shot, set shot, jump shot, etc.) or from a moving shot off a dribble (mainly the jump shot). The jump shot is by far the most deadly from either position.

We use a chart to help us determine what are the least effective percentage techniques of each offensive opponent. The chart includes the type of shot used, the type of moves used (some examples are the fake shot and drive, rocker step, reverse, dribbling crossover), the direction of the move, and the success of the move. We list the player's best move, best direction, and his pivot foot on the chart. The player must be scouted several times to determine these, but this information can become a cumulative file for returning players.

HOW TO DEFEND AGAINST THE ALL-IMPORTANT FIRST STEP: FRONT FOOT TO PIVOT FOOT STANCE

When the attacker with the ball still has his dribble, we like our defensive man's advance foot to correspond with the pivot foot of the offensive man. We have found that this limits the offense from three possibilities (shoot, direct drive away from pivot foot, direct drive toward pivot foot) to one possibility (direct drive away from pivot foot). Experience has shown us that most right-handed shooters use their left foot as their pivot foot; that most left-handed shooters use their right foot as their pivot foot.

As we wrote before, we begin with the belief that the defensive man has the advantage. We think the defender can make the offensive man move in the direction the defense wants. To dictate to his opponent, the defensive man must be able to use both the staggered and parallel stances. He must know both and dominate in both.

The staggered stance, front foot to pivot foot, should be used before the dribble; the parallel stance, along with the overplay, should be used after the offense puts the ball on the floor. The following explains the how and the why.

To encourage the offensive man to shoot without dribbling, we will let him receive a pass about 20 feet from the basket, then play him with a parallel stance, head to head, about four feet from him. The offensive man sees that he has an easy standing still shot. Then when he jumps, we try to make him raise his shot by going up with him, being careful of the fake-shot, drive move. Most everyone we play against can shoot better than 20% standing still; and under those conditions, we would not allow the easy shot.

We are now faced with how to make the offense put the ball on the floor. This depends on the most effective direction of each offensive player. We ask ourselves is he more effective going one way, or is he just as effective going either way?

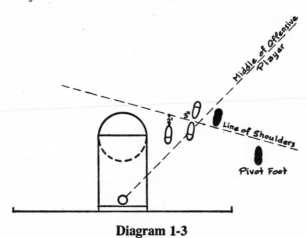

Diagram 1-3

Let us first consider making him go one way. Let us say he uses his left foot for a pivot foot and we want to force him toward his pivot foot which would be to his left (Diagram 1-3). We overplay toward his right about one half a man with our front foot toward his pivot foot but about 3″ away and our left foot (rear foot) about two feet away from his right foot. In other words we are in a staggered stance. If the attacker went to his right, we would draw the charge or we would cut him off as he veered to the outside on his drive toward the bucket. He is discouraged from the jump shot by our closeness to the line parrallel with his shoulders (3″ away). From this defensive position the offensive player will probably take that all important first step toward his pivot foot with a dribble. Once he starts in the direction we want him to go we play a parallel stance, head to head, with the eyes on the ball. Since today's ball players are well adept at going in both directions, we do very little forcing toward the pivot foot.

We limit the opponent to one choice by forcing him away from his pivot foot or in this case to his right (Diagram 1-4). We use this method also to force the offensive man in one direction when he is effective going both ways. In almost all games and against almost all modern day players, we force the attacker away from his pivot foot. To accomplish this, we play our front foot against his pivot foot (3″ away). The attacker cannot bring his right foot back over in front of his left foot

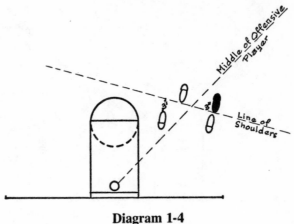

Diagram 1-4

without being tied up both by our front foot and our low trail hand position. So if he wishes to go toward his pivot foot, he must turn his back on us. When we are double-teaming, we try to force our opponent to reverse. If we are not double-teaming, then we play this back move very aggressively (Diagram 1-5).

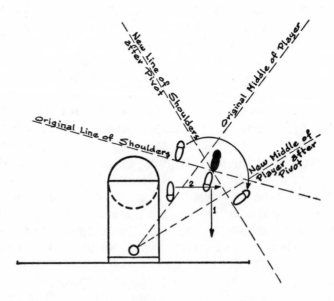

Diagram 1-5

Diagram 1-5 shows how we take the long one-two step for the overplay and force the offense back toward the pivot foot. We also do this if we are trying to force the offense to the right. The offensive man cannot go to his right without charging, and he cannot pick up his left foot without a walking violation. He cannot shoot; his back is to the basket. He must front pivot or reverse pivot to get back to his right. Both are slow moves. Diagram 1-6 shows how we take the short one-two step to maintain our front foot to pivot foot defense on the player who has reversed and is adept at scoring going to his left as well as his right.

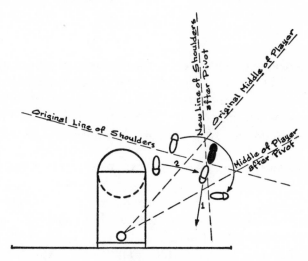

Diagram 1-6

From Diagrams 1-5 and 1-6, the reader can see that the offense will not gain an advantage on the defense by going toward his left or pivot foot. The reader can also see that the attacker cannot shoot because we are only 3″ away, and that is too tight a defense for an effective jump shot. What we have done is to make the offensive man choose to go away from his pivot foot (to his right). During the heat of battle, that move will seem to the attacker to be the one that will meet the least resistance. That is the direction we want him to go. He is now headed toward our power on defense (Diagram 1-7). We will

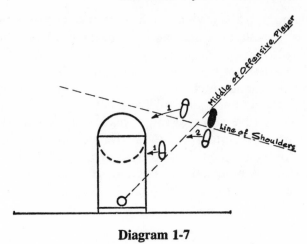

Diagram 1-7

not be beaten by the drive in this direction because our left foot is three feet closer to the bucket (the staggered stance) than his right foot. He will either charge or veer to the outside. Consequently, when the attacker begins his dribble to the right with that all important first step, we still have him stopped.

STANCE ON THE BALL DURING THE DRIBBLE

We use a parallel pressure stance on the dribbler. The feet should be pointed out and at least shoulder width apart. The athlete should be on the balls of his feet. The lower legs should be perpendicular to the floor. The angle formed at the knee joints should be 135 degrees or less. The angle at the trunk should be 135 degrees or less. The back should be perfectly straight, not humped. The head should be up with the eyes straight ahead. If the defender is in this position, he should be low enough that his eyes will be at the midsection of the offensive player, and the defender should be able to touch the palms of his hands on the floor. The defensive player's eyes should remain on the midsection until the ball is dribbled, then they should be focused on the ball and dribble hand.

The defender should be in an overplay position, about one half a man ahead of the dribbler. He should have the hand up and the foot slightly back in the direction that the ball is being advanced. His trail hand should be low. This is not only the basis of balance shown by all primates; it is also the best position for the defender to help his teammates steal a pass, for the defender to prevent a shot, and for the defender to steal a crossover dribble. If the defender's advance hand is up (shoulder height or higher), the man with the ball will throw a bounce pass. A bounce pass is the slowest of all passes, the easiest to steal. The defender's trail hand can steal any crossover dribble by being low and inside.

We use Drill No. 9 to be sure each of our players is in an acceptable stance. Drill No. 9 is a mass drill which most coaches use to develop individual defensive stance and movement. We line all players up so that the coach can see each one. We leave enough space for each player to maneuver. All the players face the coach and must be able to see him. The coach can direct many drills from this position by giving vocal or visual commands. We have three drills that we use from this mass position: stance, pat-the-floor drill, and a movement drill (forward, backward, to the sides, etc.). We use this drill to perfect stance, to teach movement on defense, and to encourage mass quickness.

HOW TO DEFENSE THE
DRIBBLING REVERSE AND CROSSOVER

The reverse is a change of direction by the offense while his back is to the defense. If the offensive ball player uses both hands to maneuver the ball on the reverse, he will generally leave the ball out where it can be slapped away by the defense. If he uses only one hand to make this maneuver, he usually draws the ball in sufficiently to prevent the steal. When both hands are used, the player is more apt to palm the ball, a violation. The coach would want to correct this in his offensive players; he would want his defense to store the knowledge for game purposes.

Two of the nine basic principles of our team defense are overplay and covering a man and a half (see Chapter 2). We use both of these ideas to defense the reverse and the crossover. The parallel stance must be used after the dribble is started if the defense is to be effective.

After the first step is stopped, we immediately go into a parallel stance with an overplay and our eyes on the ball (Dia-

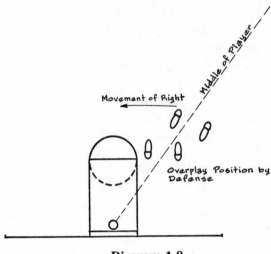

Diagram 1-8

gram 1-8). Diagram 1-8 shows the offensive man dribbling to the right and the defensive man in an overplay position. Now we must try to stop his next three or four dribbles. The rule book gives him less than five seconds to halt his dribble. If we overplay he must either change his direction or shoot. Shoot he will not do. We try to play him too tight for that. To change his direction he must turn his back on us (reverse) or dribble the ball in front of him (crossover dribble). If the defensive man is watching the ball, he is better able to pick up the offensive man's intentions. If it is to be a crossover dribble, we play our back hand down for the steal. Be careful; do not get caught reaching in or putting too much instant weight forward, or your man will be around you for the lay-up. If it is a reverse, we quickly step back and hard with our trail foot (Diagram 1-9). This is a very quick one-two-three-four step which enables us to get back into an overplay going to the left. This is how we attempt to play one-on-one defense against a man who has the ball and is located around the perimeter instead of in a pivot position.

In our team defense we try to do several things, the most important of which is to help out if our man gets beaten by the offense. To stop the all important first step or a few successive

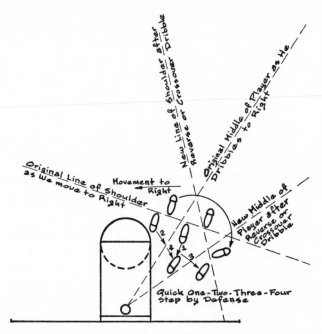

Diagram 1-9

steps is to enable our helping treammates to get secure in their positions. And this conforms with our basic team principle of guarding a man and a half.

Some coaches recommend the use of either the staggered stance or the parallel stance. To use this theory is to limit the defensive abilities of the ball club to as great an extent as the offensive abilities would be limited by using only one fake. Both stances have a place in basketball, and both are needed by the great defensive player.

Drill No. 10

Procedure (Diagram 1-10)

1. 1 can use only dribbling reverse. He may use any other fake he would like, such as change of pace, head and shoulders, to try to free himself but must reverse when he changes directions.

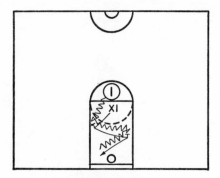

Diagram 1-10

2. 1 can change direction whenever he wishes, but he cannot go outside the free throw lane.
3. X1 must hustle into overplay, causing 1 to reverse.
4. We start drill in early season without letting X1 use his hands. We progress to hand action in about one week.
5. We encourage X1 to draw the charge, using defensive head and shoulder fakes.
6. After mastering the defensive techniques, we give the offense more area in which to work, such as the left half of the front court.

Objectives

1. To teach dribbling reverse.
2. To teach footwork on dribbling reverse (offensively and defensively).
3. To teach defense of the reverse.
4. To teach drawing the charge.
5. To teach overplay.
6. To teach defensive fakes.

Drill No. 11

Procedure (Diagram 1-10)

1. 1 has the ball and may use any fake he wishes except when he changes direction, then he must use crossover dribble.
2. X1 cannot use hands in early drill, but later we allow him to use his hands.

3. X1 must learn to cover crossover dribble both with his feet and his hands.
4. 1 cannot get out of free throw lane.
5. X1 must use defensive fakes to try to control 1.
6. After mastering the defensive techniques, we give the offense more area in which to work.

Objectives

1. To teach dribbling crossover.
2. To teach footwork, offensively and defensively, of dribbling crossover.
3. To teach defense of crossover.
4. To teach drawing the charge.
5. To teach overplay.
6. To teach defensive fakes.

Drill No. 12: Full Court Zig Zag Drill

Procedure

1. Divide team into pairs: one offense, one defense.

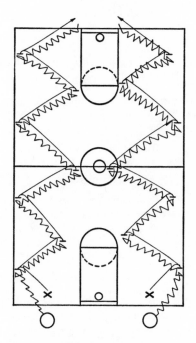

Diagram 1-11

2. The offense is to advance the ball.
3. The defense is to race back and turn the offense by use of an overplay.
4. We start season without use of hands, progressing into hand use after footwork is mastered.
5. We encourage defense to cut man off at least three times in each half court.
6. We let offense go down and back; then we switch offense to defense.

Objectives

1. To teach cut offs by overplay.
2. To teach pressure defense over full court.
3. To condition.
4. To teach advancing ball offensively under pressure.
5. To teach offense and defense of reverse and cross-over dribbling.

We include Drills No. 10 through 12 to teach the techniques of this section.

Drill No. 13: Fence Sliding Drill

Procedure

1. Players are to get down in normal fencing position, feet at right angles, hands out front as if they are holding a foil.
2. Players are to use fence slide as though they are attacking.
3. On visual command, coach has players advance, retreat, advance, retreat until they go full length of the court. Start the drill slowly then build quickness.
4. Coach must be careful that players keep their body balance (weight evenly distributed) and that their feet do not slide along the floor but are raised ever so slightly.

Objectives

1. To condition legs in normal guarding position.
2. To teach moves that must be used for pressure defense in the corner (see Chapter 4).

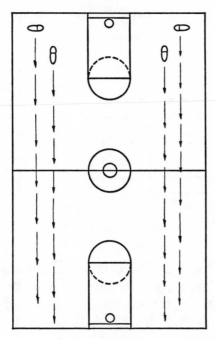

Diagram 1-12

3.   To teach visual reaction and concentration.
4.   To teach quickness of feet.

    Drill No. 13 is included in this section because it is so vital to our corner defense; and it usually takes some time to become proficient at it.

HOW TO CHANNEL THE OFFENSIVE MAN

    The defense must learn to dictate and to dominate the offense. Defense must get out of the habit of reacting to actions initiated by the offense. Defense must learn to initiate. We do this by an overplay. We have the advantage in that we know the direction the offense is to be sent, and we are three feet closer to the basket.

Drill No. 14

Procedure

1.   X1 passes to 1, then races to defend against him.

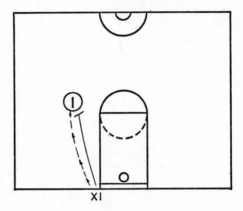

Diagram 1-13

2. X1 should use the bounce pass; it is slower.
3. X1 should alter his channeling route: one time cut him inside, the next time outside. To do this we have to have the offense switch his pivot foot.

Objectives

1. To teach slowness of the bounce pass.
2. To teach X1 to be able to approach 1 without 1 gaining an advantage.
3. To teach X1 to think defensively.
4. To teach X1 to channel 1 where he wants him, teaching controlling and dominating the offense.
5. To teach X1 to recognize instantly which foot is pivot foot of 1.
6. To teach X1 to cut offensive man toward his pivot foot. That is the offensive man's most awkward and slowest direction.

Drill No. 14 is used to develop this channeling habit. Remember we must get to 1 before he gets off the jump shot. If we do this, we can adjust as he becomes a dribbler. While we are approaching him, we must be careful that he does not fake toward our overplay and go away, or that he does not fake away and go toward our overplay. Constant drilling will limit the effectiveness of these fakes. We want to overplay away from the pivot foot while running toward the offense. We ignore head and shoulder fakes, but should the offense pick up his non-pivot foot, we will jump a step in the direction that he places the non-pivot foot, usually toward his pivot foot.

When approaching 1, X1 must always remain in motion, using the pat-the-floor drill. This will enable X1 to react quickly to 1's move.

STANCE ON BALL AFTER LOSS OF THE DRIBBLE

We encourage our defender to stand almost straight after his man has lost the dribble. We want a small flex at the knee in case our defensive man has to jump. We want his eyes focused on the eyes of the offensive man, picking up the attacker's intentions earlier. We want the arm revolving in a treadmill fashion. We want this revolving action to be shoulder height or higher. That way we encourage the lob or bounce pass—the two slowest passes in basketball. We do not want the defender reaching for the ball: this usually results in a foul or permits the offensive man to throw a chest pass or maneuver out of a difficult situation.

We want the other four defenders to cover their men tightly, eliminating any passing lanes. This can at best result in a stolen pass; or after five seconds, it means at least a held ball and a chance for a recovery.

There are all kinds of modern day offenses: the wheel, the Drake and Auburn Shuffle, the five moving pivots, the 1-3-1, the weave, the Triple Post. Regardless of the offensive system, they all provide for free-lance one-on-one movement on the perimeter. The coach who masters this chapter will go a long way toward stopping the lethal jumper.

TWO

Activating the
Nine Basic Principles

If a team could force all first shots outside fifteen feet and get all the defensive rebounds, it would only have to worry about outside shooting. The team also would not lose many games. If, however, the team could accomplish the above plus pressure the good outside shooter, it would almost have a foolproof defense. If the coach could expand such a half court defense into a full court defense, both zone and man-to-man, there would be more practice time for other phases of the game, and the defense would be of championship caliber. Our defense is designed to do all that, and what's more—our defense really develops our offense while we are practicing defense.

Eighty percent of the defensive time during any game is spent at half court near the opponent's offensive basket. That is the team's basic defense. Most of our defensive practice time is also spent there, and man-to-man pressure or denial defense is our basic defense. We have five men who concentrate on the last 128 square yards of the hardwood, and ordinarily they come out of a game well satisfied. If a team uses pressure defense as its basic defense, it is easy to change from game to game to the more passive zones.

We play our man, the ball, and an area. If that sounds like man-to-man defense mixed with a zone, it is. In today's sophisticated game, a team cannot be successful either by guarding one man exclusive of the other four or by playing a passive zone defense. We believe that the two most feared defenses in basketball are the aggressive zone with man-to-man principles (the match-up is an example) and the man-to-man pressure defense with zone principles (ours is an example).

Our defense has two major advantages over the match-up: first, a player in our defense does not release a cutter to a teammate, creating a temporary opening, a temporary break in pressure; second, most teams that use the match-up use it as their basic defense. To use it as a basic defense requires the teaching of two defenses, ours for fundamentals and the match-up.

The nine principles of our team defense are outlined in this chapter. The next three chapters tell the how's and the why's of achieving these objectives.

OVERPLAY PERIMETER

When a defender overplays a dribbler he is pressuring the ball handler to go in one direction. We predetermine that direction by the nature of the ball club we are playing and by the nature of our own ball club. We discover their nature by scouting reports; we know ours from practice sessions.

We have several options: we can channel inside where there is help; we can pressure the ball to the outside, especially if we have a big man who could destroy their baseline drives; we can channel one player in one direction, and another player in another direction in order to destroy individual effectiveness; or we can give the outside, then take it away and double-team. All these options will be discussed fully in the chapter on strategy. What is important here is the principle of overplaying all ball handlers on the perimeter.

If the attacker has not dribbled, we minimize his faking capabilities by using front foot to pivot foot stance (Chapter 1). Basically this stance forces the offense in the direction we want. Once the dribble is started, we quickly slide into an overplay (usually half a step). This forces a pass, a reverse or a crossover dribble which is covered by the individual methods outlined in Chapter 1. Constant pressure is the purpose; overplay is the principle.

DO NOT CONTEST HORIZONTAL PASSES

We do not contest or try to intercept horizontal passes unless the offense has advanced the ball to within 25 feet of the basket. Outside this 25 feet area the cross court pass is not an attacking pass, and to contest those passes would only rob us of one of our zone men, the guard not covering the ball. Contesting horizontal passes would, therefore, weaken our interior defense. The inside, not the outside, is the area of victory or defeat.

Do not worry about pressuring the shooter outside the 25 feet area. A team will not often get beat by this shot.

CONTEST VERTICAL PASSES

We contest all vertical passes, even in our full court press, except when a team has an ineffective half court corner game. The complete denial of a pass from a guard to an effective foward is mandatory. By this harassing move, the defense can completely disrupt the offensive attack before it begins. Most teams use this first pass to trigger their offense. When their corner men cannot harm us, not to contest only permits more zoning help for the guards and post men.

This is where the fencing sliding drill really helps (Drill No. 13). That is our contesting or denial stance on the effective corner men.

We never allow the pass to a post or pivot man (Red Light District). We immediately bench the man who does not concentrate well enough to accomplish this objective. An advance of the ball into the Red Light District means an easy shot for the offense. This will be the death blow to the team's pressure defense; it must not be tolerated.

SOME PLAY MAN; OTHERS PLAY ZONE

Every defender is responsible for his man, and every defender is responsible for playing a zone. We judge who does which by the position of the ball with relation to the defender.

In general, if a player is on the side of the court where the ball is (strong side), he plays man-to-man; if he is on the side away from the ball (weak side), he zones it.

That is really the importance of Drill No. 14. A quick pass back to the weak side might cause a quick move as illustrated by X1 sliding toward 1 in Drill No. 14. Mastery of this drill is imperative if our zone men are to be competent.

Zone men must use proper vision. The defender should look at a point somewhere between his man and the ball. Using peripheral vision, he can concentrate on both. A correct position should be a jump step toward and one step in per pass.

Our defenders who are using man-to-man principles must be situated according to our pressure defensive stances (front foot to pivot foot, parallel overplay, fencing or denial, and inside). The pressure stance that the defender uses is determined by his man's position on the court and by his man's position in relation to the ball.

PLAY DEFENSE ON A MAN AND A HALF

Every defender is responsible for his own man and one half of another. That is our way of stressing two things: (1) that every defender should help his teammates, especially on a loose offensive player, and (2) that the defender's primary responsibility is his own man.

This principle allows us to stress the fact that a defensive man cannot get help if he allows his man to shoot over his head (our pressure stances will eliminate this shot). We try to overplay each man's best move and get help from all the teammates for his second best move. The offensive man, according to the rules, only has four seconds to accomplish his move. But we stress for each man not to expect help; we want each man to do a good defensive job on one man.

STEP IN AND TOWARD EVERY PASS

Everytime a pass is made we require each weakside defender to step one step toward the pass and to step one step toward the basket. Both of these steps should be accomplished in one move. This gives us good recovery position in case of a return pass, and it gives us help position if the other man drives by his defensive man (see Chapter 3).

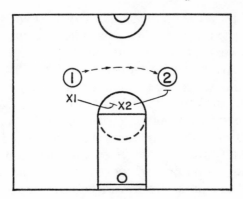

Diagram 2-1

Besides, this position gives us a good opportunity to stay between our man and the ball. The reader will see how important this is in covering a cutter (Chapter 4). And, yet, it gives us an opportunity to stay between the basket and our offensive man should the ball be returned to him. Diagram 2-1 shows a proper position as a pass is thrown by one man to a teammate. We like the footwork to be a shuffle step, followed by a sideways long jump.

SHOULD PENETRATION OCCUR, SINK AND FORCE BALL OUT

There is only one area that we protect religiously, and there are many ways for the ball to be advanced into that region. Regardless of the method of advance, we instruct the nearest man to the ball to double-team the advancer, forcing the ball back out. A rotation drill is taught to all players, eliminating the wide open shot when the ball is passed back out.

A tightly covered five feet shot is better for offensive percentages, counting the probable foul, than an unhurried 15 feet shot. Drill No. 8 helps us develop this pressure defense near the basket. Other drills that teach this coverage are developed in the next three chapters.

SCREENER'S MAN CALLS SWITCH, SLIDE OR FIGHT

Diagram 2-2 shows the ideal zones for fighting over the top, aggressive jump switching, and sliding through. Drills

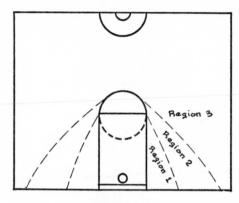

Diagram 2-2

that teach these team maneuvers will be covered as we develop team defense.

Fighting over the top in all regions, except 3, where we open and allow sliding, is preferred. We switch only as a last resort, primarily because it allows an alibi by weak defensive players. "That's not my man, we switched" is an excuse we would rather not hear. We do not permit sliding through in regions one or two because it allows the jump shot over a screen.

Frequently, we have a very aggressive and talented 5' 6" or smaller guard. We do not wish to have him guard a 6' 5" or taller pivot man. Since switching creates a disadvantage for our defense, we discourage it as much as possible.

We use a hedging drill which forces an offensive player to shift to the outside, enabling the original defensive man to stay with his man. However, should a positive screen occur, we do allow the screener's man to call switch. This means that the man being screened cannot switch because he is lazy, but he must respond to the call of one of his teammates.

ONLY ONE SHOT PER POSSESSION

Only one shot per possession means no offensive re-bounds. If every defender has accomplished an effective box out, this principle can be achieved.

We teach six different box-out techniques (to be discussed in Chapter 6): reverse pivots, front pivots, facing, cross blockouts, weakside blockouts, and wall or triangular rebounding. Each of these methods has shortcomings but when combined their strengths outweigh their weaknesses. That which is a weakness in one method is a strength in another.

We choose the method to be used by scouting the quickness in offensive rebounding by our opponent's players. We assign our man and the technique he is to use by our scouting reports and our knowledge of our players. Theoretically, if we eliminate the second shot, we have reduced our opponent's offensive efficiency ratio—one of the major ways to recognize the worth of a team's defense.

SUMMARY

From our principles and the next three chapters, the reader will be able to see the development of our half court defense. If we wish to full court press, we merely expand our half court defense.

In our half court defense, we divide the last 15 feet of the court into sections, shown in Diagram 2-3. We contest, but allow, passes into the contesting region. That area is to be covered by corner defensive men. We never allow a pass into the post region because that leads directly to an easy, high percentage shot. On the outside we use one guard to help zone inside, and we use the other guard to pressure the outside ball handler. Once the ball is advanced beyond the outside defense, we use both guards to help zone inside.

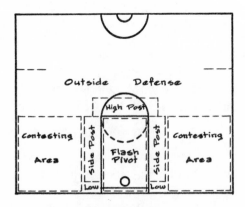

Diagram 2-3

The next three chapters discuss the responsibilities of each of these regions. Put all three defensive regions together and the team will have a championship half court defense.

THREE

How the Guards Play Defense

Every team has a quarterback, a clever ball handler. It is usually a small but very talented guard, and some teams are blessed with more than one.

If the defense is to be successful as a team, they must stop these quarterbacks or at least hold their efforts to a minimum. In order for a team to be versatile defensively every defender must be capable of stopping the most clever of these clever maneuverers. In this chapter we will discuss the methods of handling this team leader.

DRIVER ALONE

Most teams that have one excellent ball handler will run a point offense, usually 1-2-2, 1-3-1, or 1-4. The floor balance of these symmetrical offenses greatly aids the defensive guard who has the awesome job of covering the quarterback. Because of the defensive help provided by the defenders on the high wing men, the defensive guard is constantly assured of help, rarely fearing the clearout.

There are other team offenses whose symmetry is not evident, whose floor balance is not apparent. It is therefore beneficial for the defense to learn one fundamental method of controlling all the point offenses.

As a rule, we fear the driving of the clever guard more than his shooting. Because all coaches gear their offense to their material, taking advantage of the abilities of each individual, it can be assumed that a clever driving guard will be told to use his ball handling abilities to create drive situations.

If the driver is alone, such as in a point offense, he will be most difficult to handle. So we cut him toward a help that we know will always be there, namely the sideline. Drill No. 15 is used to teach this coverage.

Prodedure

1. An offensive player is given the ball at the midcourt circle.
2. A defensive man is assigned to the offensive man.
3. The defensive man is told to cut the offensive man to the sidelines, never letting him turn the corner.
4. The defender must not overplay, but he should stay about one fourth a step behind the offensive driver, keeping a cushion, thereby preventing the offense from cutting the corner.
5. The defensive player should use the staggered stance: the trail foot is the advanced foot of this staggered stance. The front foot should at least be equal and a few feet deeper than the attacker's front foot as the offense performs the dribbling drag slide.
6. The offensive player cannot reverse his direction but must try to beat the defense in the initial direction.
7. After the defense is significantly developed, we permit the offensive driver to change his direction.

Objectives

1. To teach cutting a driver to the sidelines.
2. To teach how to give the outside without letting the offense turn the corner: a technique used in defensing the point man in a set offense, in defensing the ball handler on the fast break, and in applying the double-team anywhere on the court.
3. To teach the defender to minimize the passing abilities of the clever dribbler.

When we know we are going to face such a clever guard, we usually assign our quickest and most clever defensive man to this quarterback. We play the guard with our basic stance and movement, stressing dogging tactics.

Of course we take into account our knowledge of the opposition dribbler: if we know he is not a good shooter, we encourage him to shoot; if we know he likes to go right, we force him left. We try to tilt every situation in our favor.

When faced with the difficult point offense, we pick up the quarterback at midcourt. Usually the offensive guard will be advancing the ball by dribbling, so we are in motion and ready to cut the offense toward its weakest side, predetermined by scouting reports.

If the point man approaches slowly and does not increase his speed, our defender will not have much difficulty with him. Staying in motion and remaining on the balls of the feet will be sufficient. But if the dribbler is coming at a great speed or if he changes his speed, he frequently will catch the defender off-balance and on his heels. As the offensive man approaches, the defensive man should turn and get started in the same direction as the dribbler is going. The defender should be in a staggered stance with the trail foot as the advanced foot. The defense would then try to crowd the offense to the side line, and, if possible, force the offense out of bounds.

All veteran coaches have observed a common fault among the experienced as well as the inexperienced defensive basketball player who is faced with covering a driving guard: they will reach in with one hand and try to bat the ball away. Not only does this cause the defensive man to lose his balance, but he usually fouls the offensive driver. If the defensive guard would simply maintain the proper position and be in motion, the dribbler is not very dangerous. It is only a matter of seconds until the dribbler must stop, pass, or shoot under adequate pressure.

This same type of coverage, along with delaying tactics, should also be used against an offensive guard who is leading a fast break.

In case of a clearout for this driver, we always force him away from the key, toward the sideline, unless the offense clears one complete side of the court. In the latter case we will cut the offensive dribbler to the key on his isolation moves, where we can expect help. The defender on the ball always knows where help is: we require constant communication by use of the word "help."

CUT TO INSIDE OR CUT TO OUTSIDE

If the opposition has a tendency to favor a point offense, we will cut the offense outside; if the opposition has any other front, we cut to the inside. The reasons are simple. With a two or more guard front, counting high wing men as guards, we have enough help by our zone men that we do not fear the lane drive. So we cut the two or more guard front inside. Cutting to the outside is weaker because there is no defensive help, except the immovable sidelines, but cutting to the outside is more effective when double-teaming, more effective when facing a point offense.

So a sound defensive team, one that is versatile, must be accomplished at both cutting to the inside and cutting to the outside. Drill No. 16 serves well to instill this habit.

Procedure

1. An offensive man begins at his defensive foul line and dribbles at full speed.
2. When the offense reaches half court, the coach, who is standing behind the dribbler, signals the defense which way to cut the offense.
3. The defender is in motion, using the pat-the-floor drill.
4. The defender must cut the offensive man in the direction the coach has signaled.
5. The defender is to cut the offensive man out of bounds before he can turn the corner. The defender can do this by staying one fourth a man behind the dribbler, using quick shuffle steps. The defender must also use the proper cushion so that he will not get beaten. The proper cushion varies directly with the speed of the two men involved.
6. At first the offensive man is not allowed to reverse his direction; but, when the defense becomes proficient, we permit change of direction.

Objectives

1. To teach stopping a driver on a fast break.
2. To teach visual concentration.
3. To teach defense how not to allow offense to turn the corner.
4. To teach cutting inside or outside.
5. To teach full speed ball handling in both directions.
6. To teach defense to stay in motion—use parallel stance until the defense decides which way to cut the offense, then slide with the trail foot as the advanced foot in a staggered stance.
7. To teach defender how to delay an offensive man who is advancing the ball on a fast break (this is used after the offense is allowed to change directions).

We determine the direction of the channeling by scouting, by knowing our players, and by the strategy for the game. Ordinarily, we cut to the inside because it is toward the strength of our zone defense.

There have long been arguments between coaches as to the best direction to channel the offense. We contend that great defensive ball clubs must handle both; that it is advantageous to the defense to cut some teams one way and other teams the other way.

CLOSING THE GAP

We have two simple, easy to learn, but extremely effective maneuvers—hedging and closing the gap—which make our guard defense stronger. These two are not only evident in one of our basic principles, covering a man and a half, but they are taught in many of our team drills.

All players must know how to close the gap on potential drivers. Regardless of the defense a team employs, it will be called upon many times during a game to close the gap. The farther out from the basket that a team can successfully close the gap, the stronger and more effective its defense will be. Drill No. 17 shows this maneuver. It is a rough drill, and should be taught very early in the year so that injuries, if any, will heal.

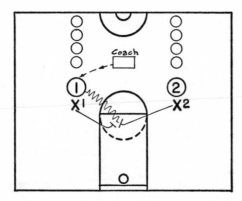

Diagram 3-1

Procedure

1. Line players up in two lines at midcourt.
2. Put a defensive man on first man in each line.
3. At the end of drill, defensive men rotate to end of line, offensive men become defense, and the next men in line become offense.
4. Both defensive men are initially covering half a man to the outside: in other words, in an overplay cutting the offense to the inside.
5. Coach tosses the ball to either offensive man—for discussion the pass is made to 1.
6. The offside defensive guard, X2 in this case, must take the quick step in and toward the pass (a basic principle).
7. The offensive man with the ball immediately drives to the inside.
8. The offside defender, X2, must get both feet on the floor ready to draw the charge. If 1 continues his dribble (offense in this drill must continue his drive), X2 closes the gap and draws the charge.

Objectives

1. To teach closing the gap.
2. To teach drawing the charge, not blocking.
3. To teach the step in and toward each pass principle.

4.   To teach visual reaction—as coach passes the ball
the offside defender is moving.

To be in position to draw the charge, a defensive player
must have both feet on the floor before contact. The defender,
ideally, should take the blow in the torso. To protect the defender have him put both arms in front of his body, one at
waist level, one at chest level. The defensive man should be on
the balls of his feet, patting the floor. At the exact moment of
contact, the defender should push backward off the balls of his
feet, letting his legs fly out. He should land on his buttocks
about three feet from the foul. He should raise his top leg in a
semi-bent position as he rolls on his side. This prevents injury
if a big man falls on a small guard. Mastery of this technique is
a must for any team wishing to run an aggressive defense. We
draw many charge violations per game, yet we rarely have
anyone injured.

HEDGING

Hedging can possibly be classified as a defensive fake
performed by a teammate of the defender guarding the ball. It
is the art of forcing a cutter or a driver to veer outside, to
momentarily pause, or to pass the ball without the defense
really having a good position. Its soundness lies in the fact that
a defender who has hedged not only can help his teammate,
but he can recover on his own man adequately enough to
prevent the offense from gaining an advantage. Hedging is
truly the man and a half principle at work.

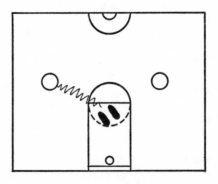

Diagram 3-2

To hedge, the defender should be sideways in relation to his man, facing the ball (Diagram 3-2). Diagram 3-2 shows the feet facing the ball, yet the defender's offensive man still in his peripheral view. It is a good position for the hedger to reach in for the steal as the driver goes by, and for the hedger to recover on his own man in case of a return pass. The ultimate intention of the hedge is to prevent the switch, as the reader will observe in later chapters. Hedging is also used on a man who is driving his defensive man into a pick (see guard-center relationship in this chapter and Chapter 5).

BODY CHECKING

On the weakside, away from the ball, a good defensive ball club will body check all cutters. By virtue of our principle of sinking a step in and toward every pass, our defenders are in a perfect position to body check. The idea is to beat the cutter to a spot and draw the charge if he continues cutting. This throws off his timing and discourages him from cutting again.

To achieve body checking, the defender needs to have good defensive position and let the cutter bump him. To do this legally, the defender needs to be ever alert to beat the offensive cutter to the advantageous offensive spot. The defender does not have to have the good defensive position that he must have to draw a charge. We have averaged little better than one foul per game on body checking. Usually it is ruled, as it should be, incidental contact or charging.

Body checking does not have to involve torso contact; arm contact will do. Its purpose is to throw off the timing of the cutter; and, if it is a patterned offense, to throw off the timing of the next several cuts, forcing the offense to re-set. On occassions, a body check will cause the cutter to stop; and, perhaps a lead pass has already been directed into the cutter's route, causing a turnover.

COVERING THE BASIC MOVES OF THE
DRIVER AND THE HELPER

The best offense against our defense is still the two guard front. For discussion purposes we label the guard with the ball the driver, and we call the other offensive guard the helper. Excluding screening for each other and other two-men plays, which will be covered in Chapter 7, these two can put into operation the basic drive moves: drive and pass to helper for shot, drive and pass to helper cutting backdoor, drive and pass to helper who will drive after receiving pass, and drive plus helper cutting behind the driver.

DRIVER PLUS THE HELPER SHOOTING

There are four things the guard with the ball may do. He may immediately drive to the outside, away from the other guard (this will be covered in guard-forward relationship, this chapter). We do not feel he will do this often because of our overplay, cutting the offense to the inside. He may jump shoot, which we do not think he will do because of our pressure defense on individuals around the perimeter (see Chapter 1). This leaves us with his other two options: drive into the guard-to-guard pocket and jump shoot or drive into the pocket and pass off.

When he drives into the pocket, our offside guard hedges toward the driver, slowing him down, allowing his defensive man to catch up and to apply the brakes. When the attacker goes into the air for the shot, we try to make him arch it higher, shoot it more quickly to throw the shot off target. When we go into the air on defense, it is only after the offense has left his feet. We then try to put our hand on the ball, making the offense raise the shot or shoot more quickly.

Sometimes, depending on the shooting ability of the driving offensive player, we will double-team this driver-shooter, forcing the pass to the other guard (helper). Many times we will then shoot the gap by a forward and try to steal this pass. We would use a rotation in case the pass is completed, eliminating the open man.

Ordinarily, should the driver elect to continue his drive, our offside guard, who is zoning it (a basic principle), will either steal the ball, or he will draw the charge by closing the gap. Drill No. 18 is used to teach all of the above possibilities.

Procedure

1. The line-up is the same as in Diagram 3-1.
2. The rotation is the same as in Drill No. 17.
3. As in Drill No. 17, let's let the coach pass to 1. This time, however, X2 hedges.

4. If 1 drives by X2, he reaches in for the steal or the tie up.
5. X2 should make hand, head, shoulder and feet fakes to slow 1 down or to make him stop.
6. Should 1 pass to 2, X2 races in shuffle steps back to cover 2 while X1 takes the step in and toward the pass.
7. We sometimes allow X1 and X2 to double-team with another defender, X3, shooting the gap for a steal. We also allow X2 to hedge, then gamble on stealing the pass to 2.

Objectives

1. To teach hedging.
2. To teach offensive passing under pressure.
3. To teach visual reaction.
4. To teach approaching a new man from our zone position—X2 approaching 2 after pass from 1 (see Drill No. 14).
5. To teach double-teaming tactics.
6. To teach coverage of a man and a half principle (weakside guard helping on 1 yet covering his own man 2).

The other alternative the driving guard has is to pass the ball back to the open man (helper). The open guard has three options: he may stay still for a pass and a jump shot, he may go behind the driver, or he may backdoor his own man. We drill on all three options until we perfect our defense.

If the open guard (helper) decides to stay for the pass and go for the jump shot, we will rush back at him with our offside guard, forcing the offense to drive back toward the congested area, where there is another pocket (help). We try to reach the man almost as he is receiving the pass, playing him tight with front foot to pivot foot defense. Drill No. 19 illustrates our method of challenging these moves.

Procedure

1. The line up and the rotation is the same as in Diagram 3-1 and Drill No. 17.
2. Again, for discussion sake, the coach passes to 1, who dribbles into the center.

3. Upon receiving the pass from 1, 2 may jump shoot or begin his drive.
4. X2 wants to cut 2 to an area on the court where there is defensive help (another defensive pocket).
5. 1 may stay where he is, back out, go to corner, etc.—this forces X1 to adjust his position and to communicate with X2, so that X2 will know where help is.
6. The first few times we run this drill we require 1 to stay out front after he passes to 2.
7. 2 can cut backdoor as 1 begins his drive. This puts added pressure on X2. He must help stop 1, but prevent 2 from having a successful backdoor cut.

Objectives

1. To teach visual concentration.
2. To teach X2 to stop 2's immediate jumper after receiving pass from 1.
3. To teach communication between X2 and X1.
4. To teach step in toward basket and step toward pass principle.
5. To teach offensive maneuvering between two guards.
6. To teach coverage of a man and a half principle.
7. To teach the defender how to approach a weakside attacker who has received a pass from the strong side. Remember if we can force the bounce pass, we will have ample time to recover on the open man. Drill No. 14 was the first drill used to challenge the weakside man who has received a pass from the strong side.
8. To teach coverage of a backdoor cut while helping cover a driver.

DRIVER PLUS HELPER CUTTING BACKDOOR

This is the most dangerous option the defense faces because there is no defensive help should the driver's helper receive a pass on the backdoor cut. Fortunately, this is also the most difficult option for the offense to complete successfully.

We open slightly toward the driving guard, constantly

jabbing and faking toward the driver to slow him down. This hedging move enables the driver's defensive man to catch up, and it also provides us with a better recovery opportunity for defense on the backdoor cutter (helper).

The foot movement of the defender on the helper resembles our Drill No. 13. It is a fence sliding move. Diagrams 3-3 and 3-4 show the footwork. X2's left foot is constantly jabbing toward 1 as we fence backward. When 2 leaves X2's field of vision, X2 opens to the ball and continues coverage on 2 by feeling the body pressure of 2, or if the officials will allow it, this pressure can be the hand tag-release method. That way X2 is already in foot position to close to 2 regardless of the direc-

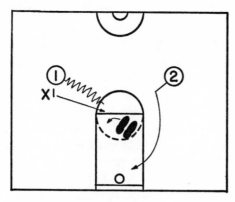

Diagram 3-3

Diagram 3-4

tion 2 cuts. If 2 cuts right, we pivot on our right foot; if 2 cuts left, we pivot on our left foot. Diagram 3-4 shows 2 cutting to his right and the accompanying pivot. We are in our denial defensive stance on 2 (fence stance), and X1 has fully recovered on 1.

Drill No. 19 is also used to teach this coverage. We simply allow 2 to fake to the middle then cut backdoor as 1 drives on X1. All the techniques must be studied closely by the coach until each player has mastered them.

DRIVER PLUS HELPER DRIVING
AFTER RECEIVING PASS

This gives us an offensive player driving into a pocket, then passing. Immediately after receiving the pass, the new dribbler is cut into another pocket. In order to stop these maneuvers, we must constantly be closing the gap. To close the gap successfully we must always channel the offensive player where there is help. To find where the help is, the defenders must be in constant communication. Communication, therefore, is the key to stopping all drivers.

Drill No. 20 explains our efforts in instilling this defensive mechanism. As you will note, this leads into some of the responsibilities of the corner men. However, we do not assume our denial stance on the corner man until later. We gradually and progressively build our defense, being sure of it by tournament time.

Procedure
1.   The line up and rotation is the same as in Drill No. 17.
2.   The coach passes the ball to 1 who drives in any direction.
3.   X1 cuts 1 toward X2; as soon as 1 is stopped, he passes to 2.
4.   1 locates at a new spot on the floor; X1 must tell X2 where 1 is by saying "help."
5.   X2 cuts 2 toward the new position of X1.
6.   1 and 2 keep changing their position on the court until they get an easy shot or are stopped.

Objectives

1. To teach visual concentration.
2. To teach defense the art of channeling.
3. To teach man and a half defense.
4. To teach recovery on one's own man after helping a teammate stop his.
5. To teach defensive communication.
6. To teach the principle of step in and toward every pass.
7. To teach closing the gap.

DRIVER PLUS HELPER CUTTING BEHIND

The helper could elect to go behind the driver. In this case, if it is a tight maneuver, we use the aggressive jump switch. If it is a loose behind cut, we fight over the top (both of these maneuvers are really part of the two man game, and they will be discussed fully in Chapter 7). In either of the two cases, we have a better than average percentage of stopping the deadly jumper. Drill No. 21 is excellent in teaching this coverage.

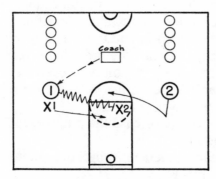

Diagram 3-5

Drill No. 21

Procedure

1. Line players up as in Drill No. 17 and rotate the same.

2. As 1 drives into center, 2 dips and cuts behind 1. 1 tries to execute the dribbling screen.
3. Should it be a good screen, X1 calls out "switch," and X1 and X2 execute the aggressive jump switch.
4. If 1 does not set a good screen, X1 yells "fight"—the cue for X2 to fight over the top. If X2 has hedged properly and X1 is aggressive enough, X2 should be able to go over the top.
5. If the defense has forced the offense outside 25 feet, we permit X1 to open up and let X2 "slide" through.
6. Instead of going behind 1, 2 can cut backdoor as 1 drives. This puts additional pressure on X2. He must help stop 1, but prevent 2 from cutting backdoor successfully.

Objectives

1. To teach visual concentration and reaction.
2. To teach the defense to channel the offense.
3. To teach "fight," "slide," and "switch."
4. To teach the aggressive jump switch.
5. To teach defensive communication.
6. To teach the man and a half defense.
7. To teach step in and toward each pass.
8. To teach offense the dribbling screen, and the correct movement to roll and receive the pass back.
9. To teach defense proper coverage of the dribbling screen or weave offense.
10. To teach the offense the purpose and the advantage of the dip.
11. To teach coverage of backdoor cutter while helping on a driver.

HOW TO EXECUTE THE AGGRESSIVE JUMP SWITCH

Diagram 3-6 shows X1, having called the switch to alert X2 to the situation, jumping out in front of 2 into an overplay. By jumping out in front of the dribbler, we mean taking one quick step up with the outside leg. This forces the dribbler either to go outside, pick up the ball, reverse direction, or charge. None of the four are attacking moves by the offense.

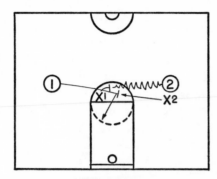

Diagram 3-6

X2 should have immediately dropped a step behind 1, a move he can definitely accomplish on a dribbling screen (Diagram 3-6). But on a set screen X2 might get caught high on 1 and be behind 1 on his roll to the bucket. Mental and physical hustle can solve this disadvantage to the defense.

Diagram 3-7 shows X2 racing to get between 1 and the ball (another of our basic principles). We also require our zone men to get into 1's path, as a method of jamming up the offense. Many times we draw the charging foul on this maneuver.

The only time a passing lane is open is at the exact moment of the switch. A delay in passing to the roller aids the defense. A couple of charges early and the offense will be reluctant to screen and roll again (see Chapter 7 for screen and roll coverage).

Diagram 3-7

ROTATION

Rotation is a key to the success of any defense. It is used to switch to a loose man, and in rotating the other four players, to eliminate the open man. If a defensive player is not taught to rotate, the good passing opponents will get many lay-ups they should not get. We begin our teaching of rotation with two guards and a pivot man. We continue it through forwards, center, and team rotation drills.

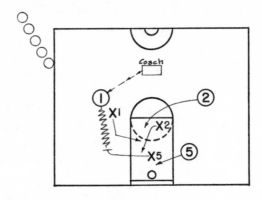

Diagram 3-8

Procedure

1. Line players up as shown; rotate from 1 to X1 to 2 to X2 to 5 to X5 to end of line.
2. The man who receives the pass is to drive immediately toward the bucket.
3. The defender on the pass receiver is to let the offensive player drive without any defense.
4. The defensive players are to read the situation and to rotate their coverage.
5. In the case shown above, the coach passes to 1, 1 drives, X5 rotates to take him, X2 sinks and covers 5. X1 rotates to 2, the farthest man from the bucket.
6. We start the drill by requiring the offensive men without the ball to remain stationary; then we begin to let them move; then we go three on three with anything goes. Drill No. 22 is advanced to include center defense in Chapter 5 (see Drill No. 56).

Objectives

1. To teach visual concentration and reaction.
2. To teach rotation, covering open man from basket out.
3. To teach channeling the driver who is free: X5 should cut 1 toward X1.
4. To teach defense to "read" and think defensively.

We call Drill No. 22 the Guard Rotation Drill (Diagram 3-8). We name many of our frequently used drills so that the players can quickly move to their positions. This expedites matters, and time is, after all, the coaches' most precious commodity.

GUARD-FORWARD RELATIONSHIP

The inter-relationship on defense between the guard and a corner man will be discussed in this chapter from the guard's viewpoint. In the next chapter, we will discuss the relationship from the forward's viewpoint.

In our defense, the guard usually overplays the offense, cutting him to the inside. This, along with the forwards contesting overplay on the potential corner pass receiver, eliminates much of the work needed to get timing between the guard and forward. However, we are not always successful in eliminating the forward pass although we make it as difficult as we can for the offense. Should the corner pass be completed, the coverage for the strong side guard is simple: he is to obey the principle of stepping in and toward each pass. This puts the guard in perfect position to help should the corner man try to drive inside (man and a half basic principle).

Drill No. 23 is one of our most often used drills (Diagram 3-9). In the next chapter we will name it the Forward Denial Drill. It is introduced here primarily to get our guards to learn how to zone it on offensive plays on the strong side. When the ball is in the corner, we have at least three men zoning (both guards and the weakside forward) and only two playing man-to-man (the corner man and the post man).

Procedure

1. Line all players up in one line as shown.

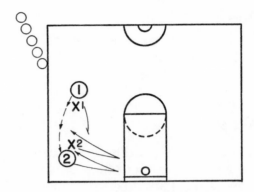

Diagram 3-9

2. Rotation would be from 1 to X1, X1 to 2, 2 to X2, X2 to end of line—new 1 comes from front of line. This way everyone gets to play each position, gets to understand each position.

3. 2 takes deep dip and X2 fence slides (but does not keep 2 from getting ball).

4. 1 should be instructed to throw the pass to 2 on the side away from the defense. Once 1 has completed pass, X1 jumps a step and a half toward pass and one step toward basket.

5. 2 goes one-on-one against X2 until 2 is stopped or scores.

6. X2 must be able to cover baseline—he will have help, X1, on all inside drives. We start by not letting 1 move, then progress by giving 1 free reign in movement.

7. We progress this drill by getting X2 to completely deny the pass to 2 (see next chapter).

Objectives

1. To teach 1 to pass under pressure.
2. To teach 2 the offensive dip to free himself for a pass.
3. To drill on fence sliding by X2.
4. To teach 1 the step in and toward every pass.
5. To teach one-on-one defense including the stances.
6. To teach one-on-one offense.
7. To teach guard to zone it (a basic principle).

GUARD-CENTER RELATIONSHIP

The difficult part of any defense is the mismatch. If the small guard switches to the big center, the defense usually concedes the score. We have a method of eliminating this switch. A lot depends upon what we call the hedging move by the center (Chapter 5), but a guard that is alert can help himself. Anytime there is a post man, there can be a pick. So we have our center use the word "post," and this alerts our guard to the potential pick. To avoid this pick our guard must learn to pull his trunk in and keep his shuffle step moving short and fast. We teach our guard to put his arm through first. He should use this arm as leverage to pull his body over the pick. We always go over the top. If the defender slides through, the offense gets the jump shot over a screen, and we wish to concede the offense nothing. Drill No. 24 teaches this coverage (Diagram 3-10).

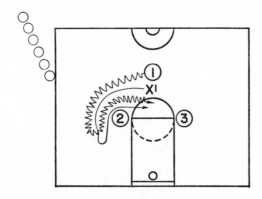

Diagram 3-10

Procedure

1. Line all players up in one line on side of court as shown.
2. Rotate 1 to X1, X1 to 2, 2 to 3 and 3 to end of line—new 1 comes from front of line.
3. 1 is to dribble until he runs X1 into 2 or 3. 1 can go either direction; it keeps X1 honest.
4. If X1 goes behind 2 or 3, 1 shoots jump shot over screen.

5. If X1 gets rubbed off on 2 or 3, 1 can drive to the basket or pass to 2 or 3 on screen and roll play for lay-up.
6. 2 and 3 are not allowed to move to pick.

Objectives

1. To teach 1 how to dribble his man into a pick.
2. To teach X1 how to avoid the pick and fight over the top.
3. To teach 1 how to jump shoot over a screen.
4. To teach 2 and 3 how to roll without taking their eyes off the ball yet being aware of charging.

The defense of this situation becomes infinitely easier when a defensive center is added (Chapter 5).

Another coverage the guard must be adept at is the coverage of the lob pass to the center. We teach this defensive technique by using Drill No. 25 (Diagram 3-11).

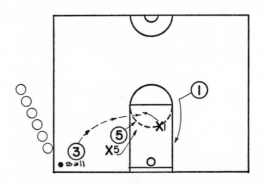

Diagram 3-11

Procedure

1. Line players up as shown—rotate from 3 to X5 to 5 to X1 to 1 to end of line.
2. 3 throws lob pass away from defender X5. 5 goes to receive the pass while X5 and X1 go for the steal or X1 draws the charge on 5.
3. Should pass be successful X5 must cover 5 and X1 drops back toward basket to try to stop pass back to

1 on backdoor cut—1 does not have to cut backdoor, but he logically would.

Objectives

1. To teach lob passing to center.
2. To teach defense of lob pass.
3. To teach center to receive lob pass without charging.
4. To teach X1 to draw the charge.
5. To teach X1 to help center (half man), yet handle his own man (full man).

The guard, who is zoning it, must be able to help the center, and yet he must be able to recover sufficiently to keep his own man from getting an excellent outside shot. We start with Drill No. 26 to teach this coverage on a man and a half (Diagram 3-12).

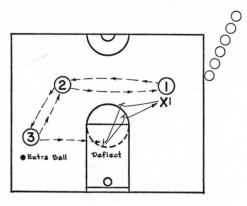

Diagram 3-12

Procedure

1. Line players up as shown—rotate from 1 to 2 to 3 to X1 to end of the line.
2. 1 passes to 2 to 3.
3. X1 sinks one step in and toward every pass.
4. 3 has two balls.
5. When ball gets to 3 he passes toward center court, then quickly picks up other ball and passes to 2 who passes to 1.

6. X1 must deflect pass into center court, then recover enough to get to 1 by the time he receives other pass.
7. 1 and X1 go one-on-one.

Objectives

1. To teach correct passing techniques.
2. To teach the sink one step in and toward every pass principle.
3. To teach guard X1 to help on passes into center yet be able to recover on his own man—man and a half principle.
4. To teach good one-on-one defensive and offensive play.
5. To teach hustling defense.

A guard must also be able to sink and force any penetrating pass back outside. We use two drills to teach this (Drill No. 27 and Drill No. 28). One of these has a one guard front (Diagram 3-13); the other drill has a two guard front (Diagram 3-14).

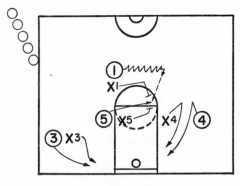

Diagram 3-13

Procedure

1. Line players up as shown—rotate from 1 to X1 to 3 to X3 to 5 to X5 to 4 to X4 to end of line.
2. 1 passes into 5 whenever he gets good position.
3. 5 immediately tries to move and X1 sinks to try to force ball back out.

4. 3 and 4 move to get open while X3 and X4 try to keep 5 from hitting the open man.
5. 5 moves offensively against pressure.

Objectives

1. To teach sinking and forcing the ball back out.
2. To teach offensive moves from center under pressure.
3. To teach proper passing off center moves.
4. To teach good coverage on potential receivers, never letting them get an open shot on pass back out.

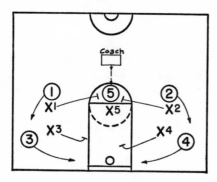

Diagram 3-14

Procedure

1. Put five offensive players against five defensive players.
2. Let 5 receive the basketball from the coach, and then he may move anywhere with it. 5 may receive the ball in any pivot position.
3. When the coach gives 5 the ball, the men near it sink and force the ball back out.
4. The other offensive men move to create different and difficult situations.
5. 5 may pass to any offensive man and the offensive man's defender must recover.
6. Sometimes we switch offensive formations from 2-1-2 to 1-3-1 to 1-2-2 etc., so we will know how to

sink and force pass out regardless of offensive alignment.

Objectives

1. To teach the principle of sinking on penetrating passes and forcing the ball back out.
2. To teach which men are to sink on which penetrations.
3. To teach the offensive center quick moves after receiving passes.
4. To teach 5 to pass from center position to open man.
5. To teach recovering on pass back out from the center.

We have discussed this from the guard's view, leaving the center discussion to Chapter 5.

When the defensive guards have mastered the techniques, ideas, and strategy of this chapter, the team is ready to move to corner defense. There are no particular demands for the guards to be tall, quick or fast. They just have to be aggressive, a tangible quality that can be taught.

FOUR

How to Defense the Corner, the Cutter

In the last chapter we permitted horizontal passes outside 25 feet to go uncontested, a basic principle; in this chapter we are concerned primarily with challenging all passes, vertical and horizontal. We will attempt to keep the forward from receiving a pass; but should the pass be successful, we will strive to keep these corner men from scoring. These defensive maneuvers are taught by a sequence of progressive pressure drills.

DENIAL STANCE

One of our basic principles is to contest all vertical passes. This means the completion of the guard to forward pass must be made as difficult as possible. At the half court game, a successful guard-forward pass usually signifies the beginning of a play pattern. At the full court level, it means the advance of the ball against a press. Therefore, we do not want this pass completed.

We start at the appropriate beginning by teaching our denial stance. The stance should be basically the same as the front foot and parallel stances except for the original positioning of the legs, feet, and arms. We call this stance our fencing stance and we begin our teaching of it with Drill No. 13.

We work on Drill No. 13 until the stance and slides become habitual. By beginning the drill early in our teaching, the players usually have mastered the stance by the time we have need for it.

In our fencing or denial stance we always have one leg, one arm, and our head between the potential receiver and the ball. On the left side of the court, the right arm and the right leg would be advanced; on the right side of the court, the left arm and the left leg would be forward. That stance is not only used at half court when denying the corner man a pass; but we also use it in our full court presses when trying to prevent the in-bounds pass.

The arm that corresponds with the advance foot is forward and completely in front of the offensive corner man. Our head is also between the ball and the corner man. That gives us leg, arm, and head all between the forward and the ball. Our weight is evenly distributed between the two legs. Our eyes are straight ahead, leaving us capable of seeing our man out of the corner of one eye and the ball out of the corner of the other eye. The denial stance is used only on the side of the court where the ball is (strong side).

The weakside defensive corner man should sink into the area of the basket to provide help on any backdoor cuts or any passes into the pivot. He has a stance that permits him to see the play develop and yet not lose sight of his own man. His positioning will be constantly changing with every movement of the ball.

PRESSURE THE CORNER

We have two methods of covering the corner, loose and tight. We may use both methods during any one game, definitely during a season.

The tight method is our favorite and most used because it adheres to our philosophy of constant pressure on both offense and defense and because most modern day corner men are offensively efficient. In this method we commit ourselves to an all out attempt to keep the offensive corner man from receiving the ball. We use our fencing stance on the side of the ball, and we have our opposite corner man play zone (two of our basic principles).

Should the offensive corner man decide to dip and come back out for a pass, we would ignore his initial step. Should he take the second step, we open to the ball. Now we are vulnerable for the quick move back out to the corner unless we can instantly regain our opponent in our field of vision. We have our eyes on the ball with our back to our man, but to help maintain proper body coverage on our man, we play tag-release. This tag-release method is not a foul because we do not hinder the movement of the offensive player. We touch him first with one hand then the other or we will feel his presence by body pressure until we have regained both the ball and our man in our field of vision. Much practice is required if one is to execute this maneuver successfully. Good peripheral vision aids. If we do see or feel the dash back out to the corner, we immediately close to the ball and continue our pressure defense with the denial stance; if we do not see or feel the dash, the offensive corner man will receive the ball. We begin with Drill No. 23 to teach the strong side forward to contest the pass and progress to Drill No. 29 to teach all forward defenses (Diagram 4-1).

We name Drill No. 29 the Forward Denial Drill because it is frequently used during the season.

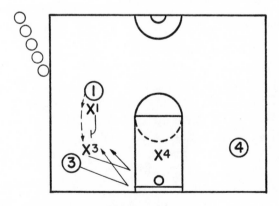

Diagram 4-1

Procedure

1. Line players up on side of the court in one line; rotate from 1 to X1 to 3 to X3 to 4 to X4 to back of line.
2. 1 has ball and may use any pass to get ball to 3; at first 1 is not permitted to dribble.
3. 3 may not penetrate further than the free throw lane on his dips.
4. 3 continues dipping until he receives the ball; X3 uses the denial stance, opens and closes to the ball, until he has mastered pressure coverage of the corner.
5. Once the pass is successful 3 goes one-on-one against X3, X1 immediately takes step in and toward the pass (zone position).
6. X4 learns to sag and help. 4 must remain stationary. X4 adjusts his position, concentrating on peripheral view of both 4 and the ball. After X4 learns to sag, we permit 4 to roam in his corner, forcing X4 to make more calculations in his adjustments.
7. We progress the drill to the point of allowing 1 to dribble out front until he passes into either 3 or 4. In that case 3's area of operation is limited to the left corner position and 4 is limited to the right corner position.

Objectives

1. To teach the offensive dip.
2. To teach passing under pressure.
3. To teach defense to step in and toward every pass.
4. To teach the fencing slide.
5. To teach contesting vertical passes.
6. To teach opening and closing to the ball.
7. To teach one-on-one offensive and defensive moves from the corner position.
8. To teach zone defense by X1 and X4. X4 changes his position as 3 makes his one-on-one maneuvers.

Two other possibilities are a lob pass to the corner man

near the area of the basket at the exact instant we open to the ball, and the backdoor cut when we are in the denial stance. Both of these possibilities are covered not only by the contesting forward but by our weakside sag. The weakside forward should be able to either draw the charge or intercept the pass. As a safety precaution our contesting forward (strong side) is constantly drilled on these two possibilities using Drill No. 29 until he makes many interceptions. Then we use the same drill to teach the zoning forward to draw the charge or intercept the backdoor or lob pass. The reader will discover in Chapter 8 that we have a defensive play or stunt that modifies the effectiveness of both of these offensive moves.

DO NOT PRESSURE THE CORNER

The other method of covering the corner is to play it loose. This is where scouting and strategy play an important part. The loose method invites the pass to the corner; and when the offensive man receives the pass in the corner, the defense still has the options of playing him loose or tight, cutting him inside or baseline. Generally we will play the corner man loose and invite the shot. If we permit the opposition to get the ball into the corner without a challenge, it usually means we are not afraid of their corner game.

We use the forward denial drill to teach this. We adjust the drill to allow the corner man an uncontested pass. The offensive man sizes up the situation and proceeds with his one-on-one maneuvers. We have found this also helps the offense decide when to shoot and when not to shoot, a most difficult offensive fundamental for a young player to learn.

WHEN AND HOW TO OPEN TO THE BALL

When: The defense opens to the ball when the offense has approached an area where it is difficult for the defender to continue watching both the ball and his assigned man. We prefer for our defensive players to watch the ball and to play tag-release with their men. At the moment of opening to the ball the defender must be in position to pivot and close back to the ball regardless of the direction the offense chooses to cut.

How: Let us discuss a corner overplay. Diagrams 4-2 to 4-5 demonstrate the correct defensive methods.

In Diagram 4-2 we have the right foot advanced and the left foot back; the right arm and head are in front of the offensive corner man. In other words, we are in our fencing or denial stance.

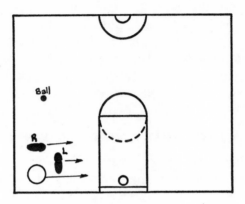

Diagram 4-2

Diagram 4-3 shows the first few steps of the offense as the defense slides backward, still in the denial stance, until the offense reaches that area where it is to the defender's advantage to open to the ball. Usually from the corner this area is on the second step by the offense.

When we open, we pivot on the left foot, swinging the

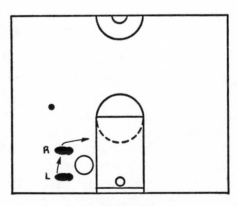

Diagram 4-3

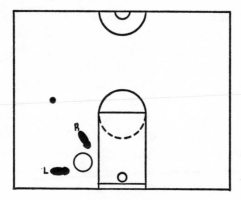

Diagram 4-4

Diagram 4-5

right foot around in front of us. Notice, we are now facing the ball, completely in front of the offensive man (Diagram 4-4). We keep in contact with our man by playing tag, first with one hand then with the other. If the defender keeps his hands on the offense the referee will call a foul; if the defender plays tag, the referee will usually ignore the contact. However, some officials call any contact a foul. Should that occur, the defender would have to feel the offensive pressure bodily or intuitively. Ideally, we would know where the ball is by sight, and we would know where our man is by feel.

This is the defense's most vulnerable position. The defender must quickly regain both the ball and his assigned man in his field of vision. Of course, if the offense stops his movement, the defender would maintain his position, fronting the offensive man, keeping his eyes on the ball, and feeling the pressure of his man. If the attacker continues his cut, the defender pivots and closes to the ball. If the offense goes back toward the corner, the defender would pivot on his left foot and close with his right. If the attacker goes up the lane (Diagram 4-5), the defender would pivot on his right foot and close with his left foot. If the forward goes toward the corner opposite the ball, the defender would become a weakside man and would operate under the zone principles.

COVERING THE INSIDE CORNER DRIVER

As a rule, we cut all players inside where there is defensive help. This is not mandatory in order to have an effective pressure defense. But should we be overplaying to cut the driver inside, we must force him as far away from the basket as we can for his jump shot; at least as high as the free throw line.

We use Drill No. 30 to teach one-on-one coverage against the forwards who drive inside. We use the stances and movement that were described in Chapter 1 to accomplish effective one-on-one defense.

Procedure

1. Line half of the players up on each side of the court; have them rotate from offense to defense to end of other line.
2. The first man in each line is to start on defense. The next man is to start on offense.
3. The offense is instructed to fake outside if they like, but once they begin the drive, they must drive inside.
4. The two offensive men are to use their one-on-one moves to try to get an open shot; if unsuccessful, they do not shoot.
5. The two defenders must learn good one-on-one inside defensive coverage.
6. The two defenders must box out the offensive men after the shot. The defenders may use any of the

methods described in Chapter 6 or use the one designated by the coach.

Objectives

1. To teach offensive moves from forward position.
2. To teach defensive control from the corner position.
3. To teach when to shoot and when not to shoot.
4. To teach offensive and defensive rebounding.

There are all types of clever opposing coaches who devise methods to destroy one's defense. One offense that has hurt us consistently is this forward clearout (Diagram 4-6).

Diagram 4-6

This pattern leaves the inside drive for the forward as a one-on-one situation. The shaded area is a lane where there is no defensive help. If we are cutting inside, it could be easy for the offense to get an uncontested lay-up. If we are playing the offense nose to nose and the attacker gains a step inside, we cannot stop him. That is one reason why we sometimes teach our inside corner men to cut the offense where there is help, and help this time is on the baseline. We therefore must have a method of stopping the baseline corner driver. Of course, a good defensive player, who has mastered the techniques of Chapter 1, should be able to dominate the inside driver. And drilling on Drill No. 30 would perfect the defense against the inside corner driver.

COVERING THE BASELINE CORNER DRIVER

Drill No. 31 shows the method we use to teach coverage on baseline drives. We have two techniques of covering it (Diagram 4-7).

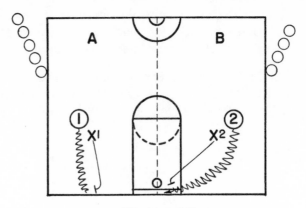

Diagram 4-7

The A part shows stopping the baseline drive by the defense beating the offense to a spot where the defender can get his body in front of the attacker and place his foot on the baseline. The only way the attacker can continue is to charge over the defender or change his direction. If the attacker reverses his direction, he will be going into the center of the court where help is, and his baseline drive will have been stopped.

Section B shows a coverage where the defender cannot race to a spot ahead of the offense. In other words the defender has been beaten on the baseline. It is unwise to think that he will never be beaten. Should he be beaten, the defensive man is in trouble. So we try to force the offensive man as near the baseline as possible. We use shuffle slides and try to keep our body even with the attacker's. We try to line our shoulders up parallel to the baseline, and our shuffle steps are quick, short, well-balanced slides. We try to at least be even with the backboard (the line through our shoulders is beneath and parallel to the backboard), causing the offensive man to jump back in toward midcourt in order to get off the shot. As the offensive man tries this jump, we attempt to draw the charge. We do not go up to try to block the shot; standing still is sufficient to draw the charge, and it leaves no doubt in the mind of the referee. At the least the defender will come out of a difficult situation even.

Drill No. 31

Procedure

1. Line players up as shown (Diagram 4-7)—a line on each side of the court—rotate from offense to defense to end of the other line.
2. X1 cuts 1 baseline, then races and cuts off 1 by placing his left foot on the baseline.
3. X2 allows 2 to drive baseline, then tries to draw charge as 2 jumps back into X2 on his scoring attempt.
4. From day to day, switch the side of court for drills A and B.

Objectives

1. To teach offensive man to drive the baseline.
2. To teach two methods of covering baseline.
3. To teach proper angle to cut off offensive man.
4. To teach drawing the charge.
5. To teach offensive man to jump back into court without charging and still score.

Sometimes we force the offensive man into the center of the court. That occurs when we know we have help there. Sometimes we force the offensive attack along the baseline (not often) where we know we always have help (out of bounds lines). If we are going to double-team, we force the offense baseline. We depend a great deal on scouting; and, again, our scouting reports dictate our strategy. But with Drills No. 30 and 31 properly taught, we should be able to handle both situations.

We require all of our players who are in position to help the defender on the ball to constantly say "help." Upon hearing the word "help," the defender can tell which direction to channel the man with the ball. Many times we prefer to let the players themselves decide as each play develops in which direction to send the driver. This encourages defensive free-lance thinking, an immeasurable aid in developing the late season tournament defense.

COVERING THE CUTTER

One of the basic principles of our defense is that anytime the defender's man passes the ball, he immediately jumps a step and a half toward the receiver. This step and a half should also be backward about a yard. This enables us to keep both the ball and our man in our field of vision. It also enables us to stay between the ball and our man, making an inside cut (give and go) impossible, eliminating the greatest advantage of the cutter. In addition, as shown in Chapter 3, it helps us form a pocket to stop the driver. This leaves the backdoor cut as the only possible individual cut. The backdoor is not a defensive sin; the give and go is inexcusable.

The backdoor is the hardest of all passes to complete successfully. Most of the time the attacker must throw a perfect pass through two defensive men, not to mention the float-ers who are drilled to be alert and to help on backdoor cutters.

The numerous cutters off screens and the pass and go behind are part of the two man game and not individual cuts. The two man game is discussed in Chapter 7.

By our principle of stepping in and toward every pass, it is easy to never allow the cutter a direct route to the ball. That is not only pressure defense, but it goes along with our defensive idea of dictating what the offense will be permitted to do. Drill No. 32 (Diagram 4-8) teaches our defense of the cutter.

Procedure

1. Line the players up as shown—rotate from offense to defense to end of line.
2. Coach passes ball to one offensive man—the other offensive man may cut anywhere except go behind the man with the ball—a give or go or a backdoor cut is preferred.
3. The offense keeps passing the ball until they get

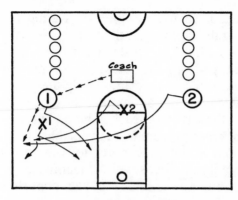

Diagram 4-8

driving lay-up either as a give and go or off a back-door cut. If any defensive man allows the give and go (the offensive man breaking between the defender and the ball), it must be corrected immediately.

4. No dribbling is allowed except upon receiving a pass as a cutter. Then the dribble may be used while driving to the basket.

Objectives

1. To teach backdoor and give and go offensive moves.
2. To teach passes on give and go and backdoor cuts.
3. To teach defense of give and go and backdoor cutters.
4. To teach driving after receiving a pass on a cut.
5. To teach driving for a lay-up under extreme defensive pressure.
6. To teach defensive concentration.
7. To teach proper defense on lay-up attempts.

PLAYING THE WEAKSIDE

The responsibilities of the weakside forward are numerous. He is taught by our basic principles to zone it. In zoning it, he is not only responsible for his own man, but he must remain constantly alert for open cutters, always thinking defensively.

While zoning it, the weakside corner man must never

allow his man a direct route to the ball. He must be constantly alert to drawing the charge on other offensive cutters who have a tendency to watch the ball instead of where they are running. He must be ready to help the defensive post man, to jam up the offense, to rotate to a loose man, to help the guards, and to be ready for many more situations that develop during a game. Experience is the greatest teacher here, but we do drill on many different types of team maneuvers that make our forward alert. Also, our scouting reports tell us the opposition's peculiarities, individually as well as teamwise.

The weakside forward has a golden opportunity to create chaos for the offense. It is not enough to explain the options to the weakside corner defender; he must be drilled on them until good habits are formed. Drill No. 33 (Diagram 4-9) is used to teach the constant movement involved by the defender in keeping his man and the ball in his field of vision.

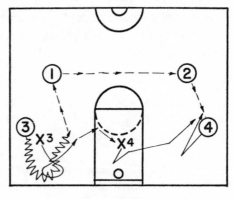

Diagram 4-9

Procedure

1. The two guards, 1 and 2, are not allowed to move. Neither is the forward opposite the ball (weakside).
2. Start the drill by giving 3 the ball—3 goes one-on-one but does not score, only passing to 1; X3 keeps pressure on 3.
3. X4 must adjust his position in accordance with 3's scoring moves.

4. When pass comes to 4, 4 goes one-on-one. X4 defends and X3 readjusts his position (zoning it).
5. The coach can progress the drill by letting 3 and 4 try their moves for a score, passing only when they are unsuccessful in getting off the shot. Do not permit a forced shot.

Objectives

1. To teach offensive corner moves by 3 and 4.
2. To teach proper corner defense by X3 and X4.
3. To teach step in and toward each pass (a basic principle).
4. To teach zoning principles (a basic principle).
5. To teach pressure stances and movements (fencing stance).

WEAKSIDE FORWARD DRAWING
CHARGE ON THE POST MAN

Drawing the charge takes courage, but it can be a game saver. Drills No. 34 and 35 (Diagrams 4-10 and 4-11) cultivate the techniques involved.

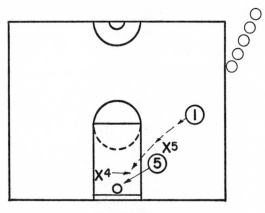

Diagram 4-10

Procedure

1. Line players up on one side of the court (Diagram 4-10)—rotate from 1 to X5 to 5 to X4.

2. 1 throws lob pass to 5.
3. X5 covers 5 in proper post defensive position.
4. X4 plays as if he is the zoning forward.
5. X4 is to steal the pass from 1 or to draw the charge from 5.
6. If the pass is completed, 5 goes one against both defenders in close.

Objectives

1. To teach proper method of lob passing.
2. To teach proper reception of a lob pass.
3. To teach pressure defense inside.
4. To teach stealing of lob passes.
5. To teach drawing a charge.
6. To teach the offense to maneuver under double teaming pressure inside.

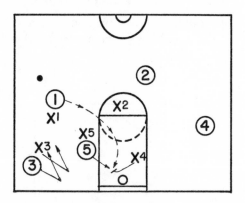

Diagram 4-11

Drill No. 35

Procedure

1. Give 1 the ball and he is to lob ball into 5. X5 plays our basic center defense. If 1 would like he can pass to 3 who lobs to 5. Upon seeing the inside pass X4 tries to draw the charge or intercept the pass.
2. If the pass is completed successfully, X5 and X4

double-team. X2 rotates on 4. X5 picks up 2 if pass is made back out.

3. Rotate the position of the players so that each can defend from different positions against lob pass.
4. As the season progresses we permit perimeter passing, but no perimeter movement. We permit the center to use his moves to get open. Anyone can throw the lob pass inside—all players must be alert.

Objectives

1. To teach coverage of the center.
2. To teach the proper techniques of the lob pass.
3. To teach 5 to have good hands in receiving the lob pass.
4. To teach X4 to draw the charge.
5. To teach good defensive rotation by forward, guard, and center so that no offensive player will be open on pass back out from center.

Pressure defenses are weakest against the lob pass to the center and passes to the backdoor cutters. Because of the extensive pressure that we exert on all offensive players on the strong side (ball side), our defense is vulnerable to these two offensive maneuvers. That is why the weakside forward must become adept at drawing the charge. It is one of our most used methods of discouraging the lob pass. An aid to our defense is the fact that the two most difficult passes to complete under game conditions are the lob pass and the backdoor pass.

To successfully draw the charge and not be guilty of blocking, the defender must be sure that he has both feet on the floor, and he must be sure to receive the blow in the torso, jumping backward at the moment of body contact.

HELPING ON INSIDE PASSES

The backdoor pass to the strong side corner man, the lob pass to the side post man, and the lead pass to the pivot man, especially the pivot man breaking inside, are all passes that the weakside corner man must intercept or discourage. The corner man can discourage these passes by overplays and by constantly being alert. We use team stunts and team rotations to baffle offenses that predominantly use these two passes (see Chapter 8). We also try to get position to draw the charge. An example of overplaying to help on inside passes and rotating to cover the vacant spots is shown in Diagram 4-11. X4 goes for the interception, X2 rotates to cover 4's man, and X5 can pick up 2. We drill on shooting gaps for steals and rotating to eliminate the open man so that we do not get hurt on completed passes but can create difficult situations even for the offense that is sometimes successful.

HELPING ON GUARD PLAY

If the coach wishes to cut all driving guards inside, his forwards will not have to help the guards if the defense plays a perfect game. However, if the coach chooses to cut the driving guards outside, the defensive corner men will have to constantly help and adjust. Under both conditions, forward help will be needed if the team defense is to be sound and complete.

Let us begin by considering the strong side forward helping a guard whose man has beaten him outside or was purposely cut outside. We begin teaching this with Drill No. 36 (Diagram 4-12).

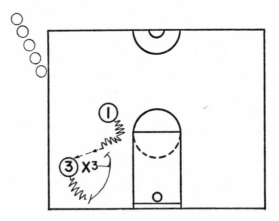

Diagram 4-12

Procedure

1. Line players up on side of the court—rotate from 1 to 3 to X3 to end of line.

2. 1 drives for basket until X3 cuts him off.
3. 1 passes to 3—3 cannot move until he receives the pass.
4. X3 must hustle back to cover 3 and play him one-on-one.
5. If 1 leaves his feet to pass to 3, X3 can draw the charge.

Objectives

1. To teach 1 to drive.
2. To teach X3 to stop a driver.
3. To teach X3 to recover on pass to 3.
4. To teach good offensive and defensive one-on-one corner play.
5. To teach good passing off a drive, almost a lost art.

Our corner man is in a denial stance on the offensive forward, discouraging the vertical pass. As the guard drives (Drills No. 37, 38, and 39), the defensive forward uses the in and out defensive fakes at the guard trying to slow down the drive. The defensive corner man must remember that his primary responsibility is the corner man, not the dribbling guard. Usually the defender on the driver can recover sufficiently to properly defend against the drive, leaving the forward to use only hedging tactics, the half man principle.

Drill No. 37

Procedure

1. Line players up on side of court (Diagram 4-13); rotate from 1 to X1 to 3 to X3 to end of line.
2. X1 begins drill by being at least a step behind 1, forcing X3 to slow 1 down.
3. X1 forces 1 to drive outside.
4. X3 shifts down to help stop 1.
5. 1 passes to 3 who tries to get off jump shot before X3 can reapproach him—3 is not to move until he receives pass from 1.
6. If offensive guard leaves feet to pass, X3 can draw the charge.
7. X1 tries to recover from his beginning position, pre-

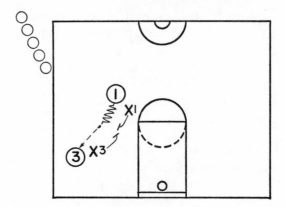

Diagram 4-13

venting 1 from getting off his jump shot—the coach
can make it more difficult for X1 by placing him a
greater distance away from 1 at the beginning.

Objectives

1. To teach guard to pass while driving without charg-
    ing.
2. To teach jump shot in corner before the defensive
    corner man recovers.
3. To teach defensive corner man to contest vertical
    pass, then help guard on driver, then recover on his
    own man.
4. To teach thinking on defense: how deep X3 can go
    and still recover on his own man.

Drill No. 38 (Diagram 4-14)

Procedure

1. The line up and rotation of players is the same as in
    Drill No. 37.
2. X1 begins by being at least one step behind 1, forc-
    ing X3 to slow 1 down.
3. 3 waits until proper moment, then backdoors X3.
4. 1 passes to 3 as X3 tries to deflect the pass.
5. If 1 continues his drive or jumps in air to pass, X3
    might draw the charge.

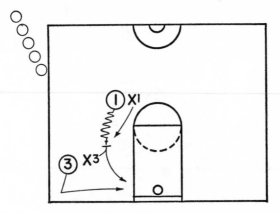

Diagram 4-14

6. X1 tries to recover from his original position, preventing 1 from getting the jump shot.
7. X3 must help stop 1, then recover to his own man.

Objectives

1. To teach guard to pass backdoor while driving without charging.
2. To teach offensive forward proper moment to backdoor cut.
3. To teach X3 to contest vertical pass, slow down driving guard, yet prevent a backdoor pass.
4. To teach team thinking on defense. X3 must be a good judge of when to try each of his maneuvers to prevent the offense from gaining an advantage.

Drill No. 39 (Diagram 4-15)

Procedure

1. Line players up and rotate them the same as in Drill No. 37.
2. As 1 drives, 3 dips and cuts behind 1 for a pass.
3. 3 can jump shoot over 1's dribbling screen or 3 can continue his drive if 1 has passed ball to him.
4. X3 contests pass to 3, then helps on driving guard, then X1 jump switches on 3's go behind move or X1 tells X3 to fight over the top.

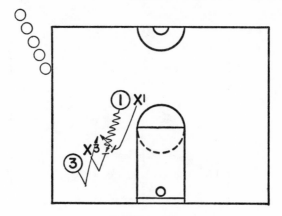

Diagram 4-15

5. X1 must announce "watch screen," then "switch" or "fight," whichever is applicable.
6. If dribbling screen is unsuccessful, X1 yells "fight," the cue for X3 to fight over the top.

Objectives

1. To teach 1 to work dribbling screen with a good hand-off (flip) pass.
2. To teach 3 proper methods to cut behind dribbling screen.
3. To teach 3 a good jump shot over screen.
4. To teach X3 not to allow corner pass to 3, then helping stop the driver, then switching.
5. To teach vocal communication and jump switching on defense.

During the hedging maneuver, the defensive forward's man probably will not remain inactive. In fact he will probably cut backdoor or go behind the dribbling guard. Or the offensive forward could stand still for a pass from the driving guard. If the defensive forward has sunk deep enough to stop the driving guard, a pass back to the offensive forward could result in an easy, uncontested jump shot. In stopping the dribble and go behind maneuver by the offense (Diagram 4-15), we use the jump switch technique. Good use of Drills No. 37, 38, and 39 will teach these three coverages.

We have other methods of defensing these offensive moves, but this leads into weakside forward's jamming up the offense and rotating (last part of this chapter and Chapter 8).

In covering the driving guard, the defensive corner man should open slightly to the ball, but always retreat a few steps toward the basket. The retreat will reduce the effectiveness of the backdoor play, but it does sometimes allow a reasonable jump shot by the forward who elects to stay in the corner. Eliminating this jump shot is one of the reasons why we prefer our weakside forward to come over and cover the backdoor. That allows the strong side forward to help stop the driving guard (see Drill No. 40) without worrying about the backdoor cut. A simple rotation can eliminate the effectiveness of a cross court pass to the weakside offensive forward.

JAMMING UP THE OFFENSE

The weakside forward, along with the defensive post man, has the best opportunity to jam up offenses. If a team has been thoroughly scouted and if they use a regimented set style of play, the weakside corner men can pick up many charges as the offensive cutters follow their patterns religiously. In defensing the nonregimented offensive teams, individual maneuvers by offensive players away from the ball can be studied and passed on to the forwards until they can be anticipated by the defender, and he, in turn, can jam up these moves as the attackers cut through the center.

When the weakside offensive corner man cuts through the center toward the ball, the defensive forward must play him as a flash pivot man, leaving the jamming up processes to the new zone men. We figure the zoning corner man can jam up the offense and still get back to his man on the weakside as the ball is being passed around the perimeter. That is especially true if every other defender is doing his job.

ROTATION

The weakside forward, the defensive post man, and the weakside guard are our most used monster men, rotaters. They are mainly our zone men. These players must be ever alert to the possibilities of rotating. Rotating is no more dangerous than playing a straight zone defense. It is not a dangerous move if the defense is prepared for it. Drills will prepare the defender; their free-lance defensive thinking will intrigue them to become more proficient at the art of rotation.

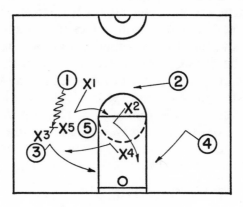

Diagram 4-16

Drill No. 40

Procedure

1. Place five offensive players against five defensive men on the court.
2. Let guards drive outside and have defensive corner men cut the guards off.
3. Have weakside corner man come over to cover 3 on backdoor cut. X4 should be able to shoot the gap for the interception on the pass from 1 to 3, or failing at that, to draw the charge on 3 who is in all probability watching the ball.
4. X2 must rotate down to cover 4 who will be cutting to the basket.
5. X1 must pick up 2, the other guard, who should have been taught to keep good floor balance.
6. If 1 cannot pass to 3, he passes to 2 and 4 moves out, then backdoors as 2 drives down the lane and coverage begins on the other side.
7. If 1 does complete pass to 3, X4 should be in position to play pressure one-on-one defense against

him. X5 could help out if 3 gets free from X4; X4 would then rotate on 5.

Objectives

1.   To teach shooting the gap.
2.   To teach rotation.
3.   To teach defensive thinking and communication.
4.   To teach contesting all vertical passes.
5.   To teach offensive driving, passing, backdoor cutting, and dipping.

Drill No. 40 shows an example of a rotation maneuver by a defensive corner man. X4 must get his body between the ball and the backdoor cutter if he goes for the interception. If he can only deflect the pass, then he may have only his hand between the ball and the man. If he chooses to draw the charge, he must do it through our previously taught methods. X2 must beat 4 to a position that would leave X2 between 4 and the ball. X1 must sink first, then race over to cover 2 should he receive a return pass.

These are not all the rotation drills we use for the defensive forward. The other drills will be discussed as we develop team defense more fully.

As the reader can see, the job of the weakside and strong side corner men requires constant alertness. Their job is most difficult. Their expertise will not come easily. Be patient and the results will become evident, and the team's defense will become awesome, dreaded by every team on the schedule.

FIVE

How to
Defense the Inside

Many coaches believe that unless they have a good center, with height, their season is useless. In our first 13 years of coaching, we have been blessed with 6′ 3″ or above material only three times. In fact, some of our better defensive teams have been our smaller ones. Our pressure defense does not depend upon having the big man.

But any great defensive team must be capable of defensing the inside. That is the area of the greatest percentage shooting. That is the area where close games are won or lost, where season records are changed from average to good and from good to great. If a team's inside defense is not adequate, it can start thinking about next year; or the coach can read this chapter, adopt its techniques, and watch the defense come to life.

When we talk about inside defense, we think of four areas: the high post, the side post, the low post, and the flash pivot, as shown in Diagram 2-3. All except the high post are in our "Red Light District"—an area where pass completions are forbidden.

COVERAGE OF THE HIGH POST

There are only three passing lanes into the high post: the two side lanes and the middle lane.

The two side lanes are covered in the same manner. When the offense sets two men out front, the guard off the ball (weakside) must sag toward the center to help on any pass into the pivot.

Our center defense on the high post man is shown in Diagrams 5-1 and 5-2.

Diagram 5-1 shows the approximate position of the defensive men in relation to a side passing lane. X1 would be playing 1 tight with front foot to pivot foot stance forcing the attacker toward his individual weakness, or with an overplay forcing the offense to the inside. X2 would have sluffed into the center, attempting to steal all passes into 5, and creating a pocket if 1 decides to drive toward him. X5 would be playing to the ball side of 5, refusing to give the offensive center a direct route to the ball.

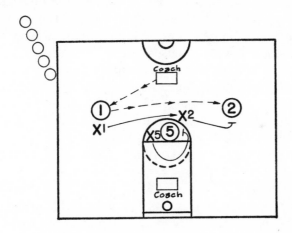

Diagram 5-1

Diagram 5-2 shows the position of the feet of X5 should the ball be in the right passing lane as in Diagram 5-1. The head, left hand, and left leg of the defensive man should be in front of the high post man, between the potential receiver and the ball. If the ball is in the other side passing lane, the right hand, right leg, and head would be in front of the offensive high post man.

As the ball is passed from one side passing lane to the other side lane (Diagram 5-1), the defender on the high post man moves behind his man to a comparable position on the other side. That is the only time we permit our defensive man

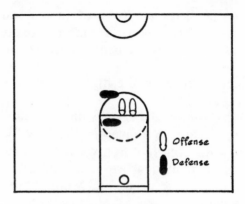

Diagram 5-2

to go behind his offensive man: the only time throughout our defensive system that we are not in a pressure position.

Whenever the ball is directly in front of the high post, it usually means a point offense and we drop our defensive post man behind the high post and sag our offensive guard squarely into the passing lane to discourage any feed into the high post. In Diagram 5-1 the coach is in the middle passing lane. If there were a defender on the coach, he would have sunk back to the head of the circle, directly in front of 5.

The only time that we will allow the ball to come into the high post is when the sagger's opponent is a good outside percentage shooter. We would then want our guard to stay close to him. Then on a pass into the high post man, the defender nearest the ball would sink and try to force the ball back out.

We use Drill No. 41 (Diagram 5-1) to teach the high post defensive footwork. We are a firm believer in footwork, and our drills on post men start with the simple mechanics of footwork and develop into the more complicated forms of team defense.

Drill No. 41

Procedure

1. Line players up on side of the court as shown. Rotate from 1 to X1 to 2 to X2 to 5 to X5 to end of line.
2. The coach tosses the ball to either 1 or 2; X1, X2,

and X5 must react to correct positioning as the ball is being passed. When the coach has the ball, X5 should be directly behind 5 because the ball would be located in the middle passing lane.

3. 1 and 2 pass the ball back and forth until they are able to pass the ball inside. Then 5 makes one-on-one offensive move against X5. 5 must make a quick move because either X1 or X2 or both will sink on the penetrating pass, trying to force the ball back out. No lob passes to the center are allowed.

Objectives

1. To teach defensive visual reaction: movement as the coach passes the ball.
2. To teach proper passing technique and form between the two guards.
3. To teach guards the defensive principle of stepping in and toward every pass.
4. To teach defensive center footwork on high post man (we have one coach checking only this foot-work).
5. To teach defensive principle of sinking on penetrating passes and forcing ball back out.
6. To teach quick one-on-one reaction move by offensive center—we teach several: drop step, power slide, crossover moves, etc. Most of the offensive footwork for these moves is taught before we teach Drill No. 41.
7. To teach defense of quick one-on-one high post moves.

COVERAGE OF SIDE POST AND REBOUNDING

To the defense, the side post is the most dangerous of the stationary areas. It is the post area where offensive efficiency is the highest. The defense positively cannot allow a pass into the side post man. The offensive side post could maneuver for a high percentage shot himself, or he could kick the ball back outside to an open man. To eliminate this pass is to eliminate the various cutters off the side post, a most difficult team maneuver to defend against.

We divide the area roughly into two passing lanes: one

above the side post and the other below. If the ball is above the side post man (Diagram 5-3), we set up above him. When the ball is moved below him, we set up below (Diagrams 5-3 through 5-6). That positioning not only makes it difficult to feed the side post, but impossible for the pivot man to move toward the ball without charging over his defender.

Unlike at the high post, however, we move in front of the side post man as the ball is being passed from outside to the corner (Diagram 5-3). That makes it impossible for the side post man to shield us from getting good defensive position by proper use of his body. If we went behind the side post man, he would get the pass from the corner man without much

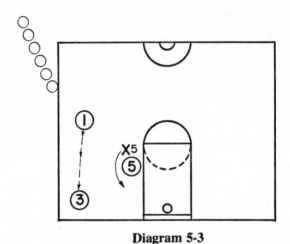

Diagram 5-3

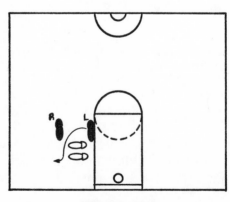

Diagram 5-4

trouble. And if he got the pass, he could easily get the high percentage shot, or he could pass to a teammate for a high percentage shot.

Diagrams 5-3 to 5-6 show the footwork as the ball is passed from the area above the side post man to the area below. As the ball is being passed the defender picks up his left foot, swinging it around in front of the offensive side post. Now he is facing the ball with his back to the pivot man, playing tag. If the pivot man slides up or down the lane, the defensive man shuffles up and down the lane. When the post man becomes stationary (as in Diagrams 5-5 and 5-6), the defender picks up his right foot and swings it around the front

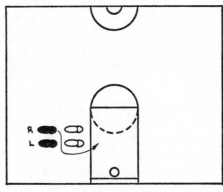

Diagram 5-5

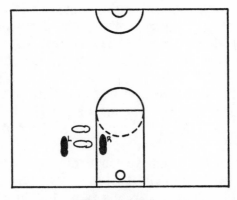

Diagram 5-6

of the offensive side post man to a position behind him. Now we are again in a pressure position, preventing the offense from going toward the ball and preventing the ball from coming into the side post man. Now let's take a closer look at some other important little mechanics.

While in a pressure position (Diagrams 5-3 through 5-6), the defensive man should put his front arm, as in Diagram 5-6, his left arm, the left foot, and his head in front of the post man. His right foot should be behind the post man.

Notice that we always keep one foot in front and one foot behind the side post man. This enables the defender to reverse pivot and box out his man should the outside men shoot.

Throughout all the maneuvers on the side post, the defender has at least one foot, one arm, and his head in front of the offensive man. Once the shot is taken, the defensive pivot man, who has one foot behind the offense, can pivot into box-out position. The only time we are in front of the pivot man is while the ball is in the air such as during a pass. Also, the reader will note that the offensive man can never move toward the ball without charging. If the defenders are to master inside defense, they must drill on this footwork constantly. For good defense, footwork must be perfected.

So theoretically, the only way the offense can complete a pass to the pivot man is by lobbing the ball over our defensive man. We try to prevent this by sagging the opposite side and alerting them to this kind of a pass (see Chapters 3 and 4).

As you recall, when the ball goes up, we try either to intercept it through our weakside sag or to draw a charge: the offensive pivot man blindly crashing into one of our saggers.

If no weakside help is available, the defensive post must try to intercept the ball himself. This is a calculated risk, but it is far better than allowing the ball to be fed directly to the side post.

Should the side post man be too quick for his defender, we would cover him by fronting or playing behind. If we fronted, it would mean the attacker is a better offensive maneuverer than he is a rebounder. If we played behind, it would mean we feared his offensive rebounding more than his maneuverability with the ball. To front, we stress playing tag, and we would probably cross-blockout for the rebound. To play behind, we would always remain between the post man and the basket, checking the attacker's moves only with body defense.

If the lob pass is giving us trouble because of excellent passing or because the offense completely cleared out the weakside, we would first consider cutting the post man baseline all the time by overplaying above him. That gives us the backboard and the baseline to help defend against the lob pass. Or, secondly, we would consider playing behind the offensive center and sinking help in front of a smart offensive center.

We use a progressive drill to teach these coverages of the side post.

Drill No. 42 (Diagram 5-3)

Procedure

1. Line players up on side of the court—rotate from 1 to 3 to X5 to 5 to end of the line.
2. 1 and 3 drill on their passing techniques until they can pass to 5—no lob passes permitted.
3. 5 must stand still at the beginning of the drill. After we are satisfied with X5's footwork, we allow 5 to slide up and down the lane.
4. 5 must learn to use his body to get position to receive pass.
5. X5 uses proper footwork to prevent reception of pass.
6. If a pass is completed, 5 uses offensive moves to go one-on-one against X5.
7. We also progress the drill by allowing 1 and 3 to shoot, forcing X5 to box-out and 5 to try offensive rebounding.
8. At intervals we either have X5 to front 5, or we have X5 play behind 5. If fronting is to be used, X5 plays tag to maintain his position; if behind techniques are used, we go one-on-one inside.

Objectives

1. To teach correct passing.

2. To teach correct methods of passing into the pivot.
3. To teach 5 to give hand signals and use of body to receive pass.
4. To teach proper defensive footwork by side pivot defenders.
5. To teach offensive and defensive one-on-one from side post.
6. To teach rebounding offensively and defensively.
7. To teach fronting and playing behind side post defensively.

Drill No. 42 is used at first to teach the footwork involved. Then we advance its format to coverage of sliding side pivot man along with rebounding, offensively and defensively.

We then accelerate to Drill No. 43 (Diagram 5-7) which activates one half of a complete half court offense and defense.

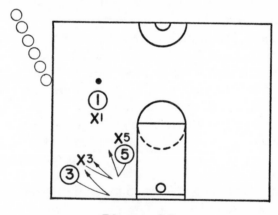

Diagram 5-7

Procedure

1. Line players up on side of court as shown—rotate from 1 to X1 to 3 to X3 to 5 to X5 to end of the line.
2. 1 has ball but has lost his dribble.
3. 1 tries to hit either 3 or 5, both maneuvering to try to receive a pass—in fact, we progress the drill by letting 3 and 5 exchange positions by screens or other offensive team moves.

4. No lob passes are permitted at first, then we progress the drill by allowing lob passes after mastering the first stage.

Objectives

1. To teach proper pressure positioning and coverage by X3 and X5.
2. To teach the offensive techniques used to combat the denial defense.
3. To teach proper team defense on the strong side, the side of the ball.

COVERAGE OF THE LOW POST

The low post is easily defended after learning the first two techniques. We do not front the low post man; we play him with the same stance as we used against the side post, covering the lob pass in the same manner as before. However, we now have the baseline and the backboard to help us. It is almost impossible to complete a pass in this area unless we are completely outsized such as 6' 10" against 5' 6".

We also use the format of Drills No. 42 and 43 to teach low post coverage. The only difference is that we now restrict movement by the offensive post man to the low post position.

After teaching the correct methods of defending against the side, high, and low post, we begin to teach another part of our team defense. We do this by using Drill No. 44.

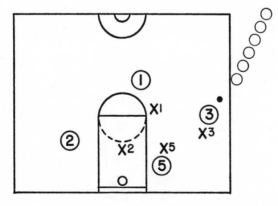

Diagram 5-8

Procedure

1. Line players up on side of court as shown—rotate from 3 to X3 to 1 to X1 to 2 to X2 to 5 to X5 to end of line.
2. At the beginning, we allow only 5 to move offensively. The other offensive players drill on passing, and the defenders drill on use of the zoning principle. Then we progress the drill by allowing the whole offense to move.
3. We limit 5's movement to high, side, and low pivot positions. After we learn defense of the flash pivot, 5 is permitted to cut through the lane.
4. X5 must cover 5 correctly. X1, X2, and X3 cover their men with correct defensive outside techniques.
5. Once the ball is passed into 5, he goes one-on-one with either X1, X2, or X3 sinking to force ball back out (another basic principle).

Objectives

1. To teach perimeter passing.
2. To teach correct team defensive zoning principles.
3. To teach the correct fundamentals of defense on the center.
4. To teach the correct defensive man to sink and help force the ball back out.
5. To teach one-on-one offense and defense from the center position.
6. To teach defense against the lob pass.

COVERAGE OF THE FLASH PIVOT

The most dangerous inside area is the flash pivot. It lies in the center of the "Red Light District" and a completed pass usually means two points. Any defensive man who permits his man to receive a pass in this position is immediately removed from the game. The coach must insist upon this. When the players see that a completion will remove them from a game, the coach will be amazed at how much more aggressive the inside defenders become and how much better they begin to concentrate. And as we said once before, concentration is a basic fundamental, a key to excellent defense.

We divide this 180 square feet of floor space into two parts: the upper bounds and the lower bounds. When the ball is high we force the cutter low. When the ball is low, we force the cutter high. The rules help us play defense in this area: we have to cover the cutter for only three seconds. Our coverage of the corner men and the perimeter area blends perfectly with our coverage of the flash pivot.

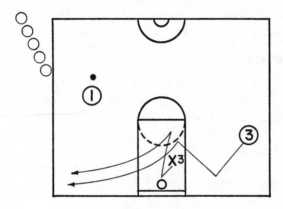

Diagram 5-9

Drill No. 45

Procedure

1. Line players up on side of court as shown—rotate from 1 to 3 to X3 to end of line.
2. 1 is to try to hit 3 with a pass as he breaks into the flash pivot.
3. X3 beats 3 to spot of intended pass and forces 3 low.
4. X3 then denies any pass to 3 out to the corner.
5. We begin this drill by walking through it. We then permit three-quarter speed, then full speed. We would allow 3 to stop at the side post and maneuver for the ball. Or we would allow 3 to come up to guard instead of cutting through the lane into the corner.
6. Now we progress by putting a defensive man on 1 and allowing any of the guard-center relationships, guard-forward relationships, and guard-guard rela-

tionships. When the defenders are competent in this drill, they should be able to handle any flash pivot forced low.

7. Anytime there is a completed pass into the pivots, we go one-on-one.
8. The drill may be progressed to a full court drill by letting X3 become offense and 3 defense on interceptions. That is good for late season conditioning and good for developing the quick switch from offense to defense and defense to offense.

Objectives

1. To teach 1 to make good passes to a moving pivot.
2. To teach 3 to receive the ball and be ready for instant fake and drive on offense.
3. To teach X3 proper methods and techniques of defensing a flash pivot.
4. To teach X3 progression from center to forward play, from weakside zoning to strong side play, from center to guard play.
5. To teach good one-on-one offensive and defensive moves.
6. To teach good guard, forward, and center defensing.
7. To teach late season conditioning.
8. To help develop fast break after interception.
·9. To help develop conversion from offense to defense.

Drill No. 46

Procedure

1. Line players up on side of court as shown—rotate from 1 to 3 to X3 to end of line.
2. 3 dips and breaks into flash pivot area.
3. X3 cuts 3 off sending him to side post region high.
4. We begin the drill by walking through it, then three-quarter speed, then full speed.
5. After we master footwork we allow 3 to stay as a side pivot, then we allow him to move out to a guard. We can put a defensive man on 1 and have a forward-center relationship, a forward-guard relationship.

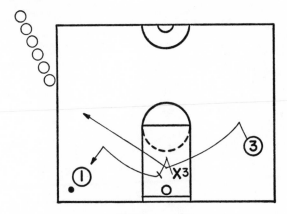

Diagram 5-10

6.   Anytime the ball is completed to the flash pivot, he is to go one-on-one.
7.   We may progress the drill by permitting X3 to drive the length of the court on an interception with 3 trying to stop him.

Objectives

1.   To teach 1 to make good passes to a moving pivot.
2.   To teach 3 to receive ball and be ready for offense.
3.   To teach X3 proper methods and techniques of defensing a flash pivot.
4.   To teach X3 progression from center to guard, from weakside to strong side play.
5.   To teach one-on-one offensively and defensively.
6.   To teach good guard, forward and center defensing.
7.   To teach late season conditioning.
8.   To help develop the fast break after an interception.
9.   To help develop conversion from offensive play to defensive play.

Drill No. 47

Procedure

1.   Line players up on side of court as shown—rotate from 1 to X1 to 3 to X3 to end of line.
2.   1 passes to 3, and X3 and X1 react. 3 is a high wingman, not a corner man.

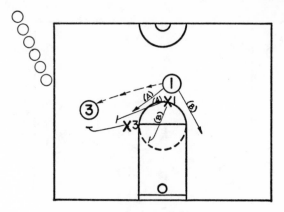

Diagram 5-11

3.   1 cuts vertically either on give and go (A) or on backdoor (B). 1 is not to cut behind 3.

4.   1 becomes a flash pivot from out front. If 1 chooses give and go route, he is a side pivot. If 1 goes backdoor route, he can re-break into flash pivot area from the side opposite the ball. X1 should step in and toward each pass as indicated by (A) and (B).

Objectives

1.   To teach X1 and X3 to react on passes (step in and toward each pass).

2.   To teach good passing techniques by 1 and 3.

3.   To teach 1 to become a vertical cutter.

4.   To teach X1 proper method of covering vertical flash pivot cutter.

Drills No. 45, 46, and 47 teach these all-important defensive coverage techniques of the flash pivot. As the reader can see from Diagrams 5-9 and 5-10, we simply beat the offensive man to a spot and force him in another direction away from the ball. In Diagram 5-9, X3 would cover 3 with the contesting or denial stance as 3 moves toward the strong side corner. In Diagram 5-10, X3 would sink and begin zoning it under the rules of guard play (Chapter 3) as 3 goes on out and becomes an offensive guard.

The footwork is the same as in the side post coverage,

plus we open to the ball the second we force the offensive man in the other direction. The defender must be careful here to keep his man in his field of vision except for the exact moment he opens to the ball. The defender must never take his eye off the ball. Then the defender must quickly re-establish his man in his field of vision or the attacker will fake the defender and receive the pass in the "Red Light District." As 3 cuts away from the ball, the defensive man is in a fence or denial stance, sliding with 3 until he reaches the outside.

Constant drilling will perfect the footwork, the moment of opening to the ball with the tagging process, and the re-closing to the ball. Remember, the offense only has three seconds in the lane.

The ball may be advanced into the flash pivot area in several ways other than by passing—by dribbling, for example. Regardless of the method of advance, once the ball is in the "District," the defensive man on the ball must cover the opponent extremely tight, and the closest outside defensive man must sink and double-team. Everyone else must sag and try to force a pass back out, a basic principal, as we would much rather take our chances with the outside shot under quick coverage.

We have two drills in Chapter 3, Drill No. 27 and Drill No. 28, that have better enabled us to sink and force the ball back out. These two drills and their progressions have solidified this important aspect of our team defense.

Drill No. 48

Procedure

1. Line players up on the side of the court as shown —rotate from 1 to X1 to 2 to X2 to 3 to X3 to end of line.
2. 1 passes to 2 while X1 and X2 step in and toward every pass.
3. 3 and X3 play corner offense and defense into pivot offense and defense, into opposite corner offense and defense.
4. If 1 or 2 can pass the ball into 3, they do. Should the pass be completed, X3 plays one-on-one defense.

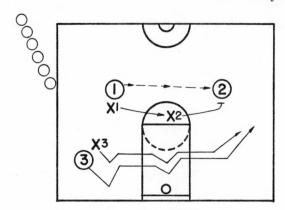

Diagram 5-12

Objectives

1. To teach proper perimeter techniques.
2. To teach X1 and X2 proper defensive guard techniques.
3. To teach 3 proper methods of getting open against pressure defenses.
4. To teach X3 proper defensive techniques on offensive corner and post men.
5. To teach good one-on-one defensive and offensive play.
6. To teach the defenders how to defense a combination of areas in one play: in this case, from the strong side corner to side pivot to flash pivot to weakside corner.

Drill No. 49

Procedure

1. Line players up on side of court as shown—rotate from 1 to X1 to 2 to X2 to 3 to X3 to 5 to X5 to end of line.
2. 1, 2, and 3 cannot move, but they must pass the ball back and forth until 5 gets open. X5 tries to keep the center from getting a pass.
3 · We run this drill for 10 seconds at a time, then rotate.

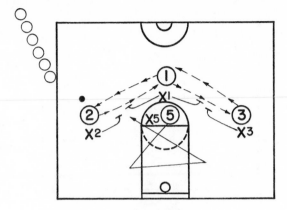

Diagram 5-13

4. If a pass is completed to 5, he and X5 go one-on-one.
5. X1, X2, and X3 step in and toward every pass.
6. The correct defender, either X1, X2 or X3, must sink and force the penetrating pass back out.

Objectives

1. To teach passing.
2. To teach the step in and toward every pass principle.
3. To teach coverage of a moving pivot.
4. To teach offensive pivot moves under pressure.
5. To teach offensive and defensive one-on-one center play.
6. To teach sinking and forcing ball back out.

Drill No. 48 and Drill No. 49 have been good to us as far as drilling on combining more than one phase of our pivot and corner defense. Drill No. 48 deals with defensing the contesting area to the post area to the weakside corner area. Drill No. 49 deals with coverage of a moving pivot, meaning the pivot changes from high to side to low to flash as ball is passed from 1 to 2 to 3.

Drill No. 50

Procedure

1. Line players up at end of court as shown—rotate

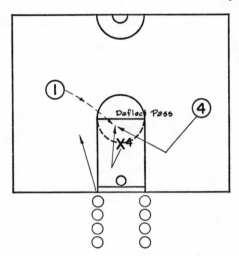

Diagram 5-14

from 1 to 4 to X4 to end of left line to end of right line.

2. 4 dips and breaks into flash pivot; X4 cuts him off and deflects the pass.
3. The two lines race for the deflected ball—the one coming up with the loose ball is on offense; the other one is on defense in a one-on-one half court game.

Objectives

1. To teach offensive dip, change of pace, and change of direction.
2. To teach defense of the flash pivot.
3. To teach defensive hustle.
4. To teach recovery of loose balls.
5. To teach one-on-one offensively and defensively.
6. To teach instant conversion from offense to defense.

Drill No. 50 is an excellent progression drill. It enables us to teach the advantage of hustle. The pass in to the flash pivot is deflected, allowing our teammates to recover the loose ball. That opportunity will happen numerous times during any game. Defensive men must not worry about the scrapes they will get from diving after loose balls. That is aggressive pres-

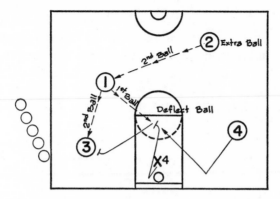

Diagram 5-15

sure defense at its best. Drill No. 51 is also a progression drill that teaches deflection of passes to flash pivots and yet recovery on a corner man before the corner man can get off his shot.

Drill No. 51

Procedure

1. Line players up near baseline as shown—rotate from 3 to 1 to 2 to 4 to X4 to end of the line.
2. 1 has a ball; and 2 has an extra ball.
3. 4 tries to break into flash pivot area and X4 beats him to the advantageous spot.
4. 1 throws a pass to 4 but X4 deflects it. If the pass is completed, X4 and 4 go one-on-one.
5. After step 4 is completed, 2 passes extra ball to 1 who passes to 3, and 3 and X4 go one-on-one.

Objectives

1. To condition.
2. To teach proper offensive flash pivot techniques.
3. To teach proper defensive flash pivot techniques.
4. To teach good passing techniques.
5. To teach inside defensive men the advantage to hustling.
6. To teach offensive and defensive one-on-one play.
7. To teach deflection of a pass, yet recovery to another attacker.

INSIDE HEDGING

Hedging, the art of slowing down one attacker while guarding another, is best used by the inside personnel. It is an integral part of our defense. We simulate game conditions by use of Drill No. 52. Inside hedging is accomplished by using the same techniques that were used in guard hedging (see Chapter 3).

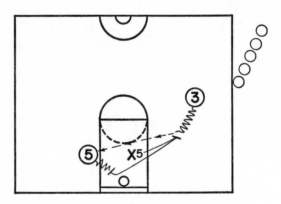

Diagram 5-16

Procedure

1. Line players up on side of court as shown—rotate from 3 to 5 to X5 to end of the line.
2. 3 fakes then drives to basket; X5 must stop him then race to cover 5, who is not permitted to move until after he has received the pass from 3.
3. X5 must really move to get to 5 before he shoots.
4. We can progress the drill by giving 3 a defender, allowing rotation and hedging with a live two-on-two scrimmage.

Objectives

1. To teach driving to basket from forward position.
2. To teach helping on a loose driving forward.
3. To teach recovering on one's own man.
4. To teach hustle on inside defense.
5. To teach rotation and hedging.

Inside hedging is developed to become a quick thinking part of our defense. We progress Drill No. 52 by assigning 3 a defensive man. Then we allow 3 to beat X3 baseline, permitting X5 to quickly switch onto 3 and X3 to pick up 5. This by necessity must be a quick switch.

We have other inside hedging drills which are of great help in defensing the rub-offs. In fact, these drills are the hub of our inside defensive hedging. Drills No. 53 and 54 show the inside hedging drill with the forward and guard respectively, but there is need to discuss the techniques, the how's and the why's.

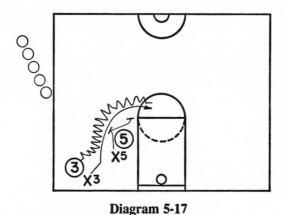

Diagram 5-17

Drill No. 53: Forward-Center Inside Hedging

Procedure

1. Line players up on side of court as shown—rotate from 3 to X3 to 5 to X5 to end of the line.
2. 3 is instructed to drive his defensive man into 5. 5 must not be permitted to move. 3 keeps dribbling until he is successful in rubbing his defensive man onto 5.
3. X5 must use the hedging technique to force 3 outside and off his course. X5 must be sure to get out of X3's way, permitting X3 to catch up to and stop 3. Proper mastery of the footwork involved will assure successful timing between X3 and X5.

4. When 3 rubs his man off on 5, he may jump shoot over the screen or drive to the basket.
5. Never allow X3 to slide through—that gives 3 the jump shot over 5's screen—X3 must fight over the top, or X5 must call the aggressive jump switch.

Objectives

1. To teach defensive center the hedging technique.
2. To teach defensive forward how to fight over the top.
3. To teach 3 how to drive his man by dribbling into a screen; then to shoot the jump shot over the screen or drive.
4. To teach good ball handling under extreme pressure.
5. To teach good defensive timing between the defensive forward and the defensive center.

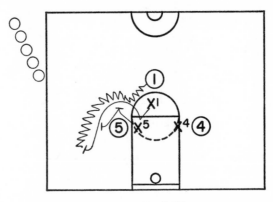

Diagram 5-18

Drill No. 54: Guard-Center Inside Hedging

Procedure

1. Line players up on the side of the court as shown —rotate from 1 to X1 to 5 to X5 to 4 to X4.
2. 1 is instructed to drive his man into 5 or 4 by dribbling. By 1 having the option of going either way, the defensive guard cannot cheat on his coverage. 5

and 4 may not move. 1 keeps dribbling until he executes successful rub-off.

3. X5 and X4 must use defensive hedging technique to help X1.
4. 1 is to jump shoot over the screen or drive for the lay-up on successful rub-off.
5. X1 must not slide through; he must always fight over the top; or X5 or X4 must call the aggressive jump switch.

Objectives

1. To teach defensive center the hedging technique.
2. To teach defensive guard to fight over the top.
3. To teach 1 how to drive his man while dribbling into a rub-off and then to shoot a jump shot over the screen or drive for the lay-up.
4. To teach good ball handling under extreme pressure.
5. To teach good defensive timing between the defensive guard and the defensive center.

The why's of this technique are obvious. Inside hedging helps prevent the center from having to switch to a smaller man, eliminating the mismatch, permitting the assigned guard to stay with his man; and, it helps to keep the big man in the center of the defense.

This technique is designed to aid the defense in four ways. First, to draw the charge—if the dribbler continues in a straight line with the ball, he will charge over the center. Second, the dribbler can pick up the ball—in which case no harm can be done by the rub-off. Third, the dribbling offensive man can change his direction back toward his defensive guard. That is certainly to the defense's advantage. Or fourth, the guard can continue his dribbling drive by cutting further to the outside. In that case, the defensive man should easily be able to fight over the top and stay with his own man. There is one caution: the center must always be alert to his man's breaking toward the basket for a lead lob pass. However, if the weakside help is alert, this lob pass cannot consistently be effective.

Now how do we accomplish this? The footwork of the

center is exactly the same as that of coverage on the side post man, except the center steps outside a half a step. Remember, our strong side center defense is always in a contesting stance, always on the side of the ball. Diagrams 5-19 through 5-21 show how we try to use the hedging move to help our guard fight over the top. The same footwork is used if the drive originates from a forward or corner position.

Let's say that 1 is trying to rub his man off on a center. The center immediately pivots on his right foot, placing his left foot in front of 1, facing 1, cutting 1 further outside. Then as 1 hesitates and cuts outside, X1 should be able to catch up and the center should be pivoting on his left foot, swinging his

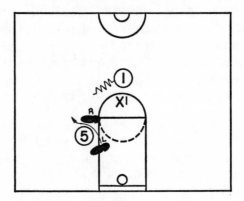

Diagram 5-19

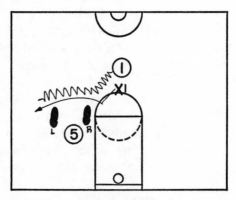

Diagram 5-20

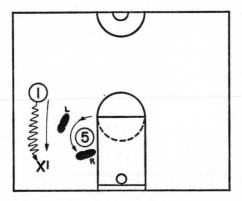

Diagram 5-21

right foot between 5 and the ball, allowing X1 to easily come hard and fast over the top. Sometimes a small shuffle step is required for X5 to regain excellent position on 5. Notice that this goes along with our ideas of covering a side post man, and it has an additional advantage in that we do not have to teach new footwork. Timing between X1 and X5 is essential to the success of this maneuver. Drilling will provide this timing.

The ideas of inside hedging can also be used to avert effective screen and roll plays, to completely stop the jump shot over a screen, and to permit excellent rotations. It does not have to be used by the big man to gain full advantages for the defense. The guards and forwards can use this hedging technique on screens and rolls or any screen play where the ball is involved. It will curb the effectiveness of many offensive maneuvers (see Chapter 7).

ROTATION

Rotation is such a major part of our defense that it has been discussed thoroughly and should be sufficiently understood. However, the center's rotation duties are so mammoth that we believe it is best for the center to initiate it. The center calls his part in the rotation by the word "rotate."

We do not believe in giving any type of easy shot. We want our opposition to become tired of not being open. Then we can destroy them. At the end of a game we want our opposition to say, "We had to work hard for every shot."

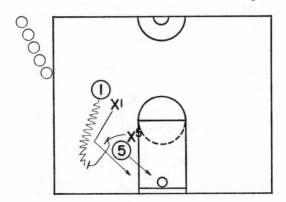

Diagram 5-22

Drill No. 55

Procedure

1. Line players up on the side of the court as shown
   —rotate from 1 to X1 to 5 to X5 to end of the line.
2. 1 drives toward the basket with X1 trailing on purpose, illustrating a defender getting beat on drive to
   the basket.
3. X5 rotates to cover the open man, 1, and X1 rotates
   to pick up 5.
4. X5 must call out "rotate."

Objectives

1. To teach good dribbling techniques under pressure.
2. To teach proper rotation by defenders.
3. To teach team techniques of rotations (guards and
   centers here).
4. To teach center to help defensive guard who has
   been beaten.
5. To teach 5 proper use of body to shield off X1 on the
   return pass.

Drill No. 56 (See Diagram 3-8)

Procedure

1. Line players up on side of the court as shown

—rotate from 1 to X1 to 2 to X2 to 5 to X5 to end of the line.
2. 1 drives toward basket (X1 purposely trailing). X5 calls out "rotate" and switches over on 1.
3. 1 can shoot, pass to 5 or 2, or drive for a lay-up.
4. X2 sinks toward basket to prevent 5 from getting a lay-up; X1 rotates over on 2.

Objectives

1. To teach 1 to make instant decision to drive, pass, or shoot: he learns to recognize his options by reading the defense.
2. To teach 5 to use body to try to fend off X2 and receive inside pass for the power lay-up.
3. To teach rotation by X1, X2, and X5 (two guards and a center).
4. To teach defensive communication.
5. To teach defensive free-lance thinking, that elusive quality known as savvy.

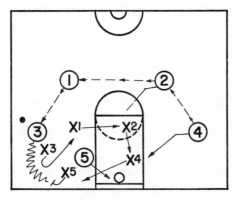

Diagram 5-23

Drill No. 57

Procedure

1. Line up five offensive and five defensive players —rotate the players' positions.

2.   We allow the outside men to pass ball around until the forwards get open.
3.   3 drives to basket—X5 rotates when he calls "rotate."
4.   X4 rotates on 5; X2 takes 4; X1 takes 2; and X3 covers 1.
5.   5 tries to get position for pass from 3.
6.   The coach can alter the drill by letting any of the outside men drive when they can beat their defender.

Objectives

1.   To teach proper perimeter passing.
2.   To teach team defensive rotation.
3.   To teach offensive driving and passing off, a lost art.
4.   To teach offensive pass reception under pressure.
5.   To teach coverage of all loose men without getting confused.
6.   To teach sink in and toward every pass principle.
7.   To teach zoning principle.
8.   To teach closing the gap.
9.   To teach free-lance defensive thinking (savvy).

These three center rotation drills have completely solidified our rotation defense. Drills No. 55 through 57, when mastered, have enabled us to virtually never miss picking up the loose man. Using rotation, hedging, and switching off tactics has eliminated the open lay-ups by our opposition.

SLOWING DOWN THE OFFENSE

The center is in the best position to read what the offense is attempting to do. With a little defensive knowledge and a little imagination the center can slow down the best of offenses. Whenever the offense has outside men cutting through the inside to try to receive a pass, the defensive center can learn the cuts early in a game, then he can move in front of many cutters, drawing the charges.

A shuffle cut offers one example (Diagram 5-24): as 1 cuts to the basket to receive the pass from 3, X5 can move in front of the offensive guard, who is probably watching the ball, and easily draw the charging foul. Failing to draw the charge, X5 would have slowed down 1's cut which would

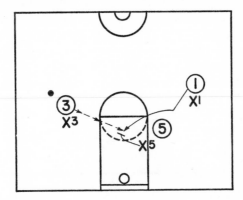

Diagram 5-24

affect the timing of the second cut, the third cut and so on throughout the entire offensive possession.

We do not have a drill on how to slow down an offense because today's players are well coached on individual and free style techniques. However, during five-on-five half court scrimmages, we frequently halt play to explain to the center how he could have slowed down a cutter in a particular situation. After several weeks, even the most inexperienced center will begin to think defensively and offer quite an obstacle to inside offensive play.

We have found that good aggressive play around the key enables us to steal many inside passes, to draw many charges, and to force many violations. It forces the offense to operate from the perimeter and thus discourages them. By convincing them early in the game that we're not going to permit an inside offensive, we tend to put the opposition on the defensive.

If the reader has mastered the last three chapters, he will have a team defense that is of championship caliber over the last 25 feet of the court. That would be sufficient to win many games. But we expand our defense throughout all phases of the game and over the entire court. We drill even further on the defense of particular offensive maneuvers that are peculiar to all team offenses over the last 25 feet of the court. The rest of this book is devoted to this expansion of the defense and to this understanding of the little things involved in defensive coverage of offensive team maneuvers.

SIX

Methods of Getting Control of the Ball

What happens in the sum total of each possession of the basketball determines the outcome of a game. That statement is elementary, but the coach cannot place too much emphasis on it. Each possession is worth three points: a field goal and a free throw. Without a defense, all offenses would record at least two points per possession. The better the defense, the lower the point output per possession. Each team will have the ball approximately the same number of times. Therefore, what happens in each possession in contrast to what the opponents do in each possession will determine the final outcome of a game, of a season.

Defense, therefore, exists for one primary purpose: to get the ball for the offense with the minimum amount of damage. There are three major ways to accomplish this primary objective: after a successful score, turnovers, and rebounding the missed shots. Each has its place in the scheme and strategy of defense. Each is discussed fully in this chapter.

AFTER A SUCCESSFUL SCORE

The easiest method and one of the three most numerous

ways of regaining control of the ball is after a successful score by the opponents. Ordinarily, this is also the most damaging way to regain the ball. If the opposition scored during each possession, the chances of the defensive club's winning would be slim.

But there are times when it is strategically advantageous to allow the opposition a score. For example, the defense has a three point lead and their opponents have the ball with only seconds remaining. To play tight aggressive defense, possibly allowing a three-point play, would be foolish. To foul, allowing the clock to stop, would be equally unwise. So give the basket and reap a one point victory.

It might be strategically profitable to allow a score by committing a personal foul, allowing a free throw, hoping to regain the ball and get two points. Of course, this is hoping that the opposition makes only one point of the one and one or two shot foul. That is especially true late in a game when a team is trailing and must have possession of the ball.

There are other times when it might appear favorable to allow a score, but, generally, this is the worst of all methods to achieve the defensive primary objective of regaining control of the ball for the offense. Allowing a score is certainly not good defensive play.

TURNOVERS

In our nomenclature of basketball we define center jumps, held balls, charging, violations, intercepting passes, forcing free balls and recovering them, and forcing bad shots as turnovers. We figure the team that wins the turnover battle will usually win the game. If a team can limit their turnovers to ten while forcing their opposition to lose control of a possession 25 times, the team has a potential 90 point advantage. That is 15 extra times that the team with fewer turnovers will try for a basket and 15 times their opposition will not. Each possession is worth three points, and 30 (15 plus 15) times three equals 90. Spot a team 90 points and see if they are easily beaten. This is an exaggeration but all coaches will agree that a turnover hurts a ball club's chances of winning as much as a missed shot, an uncovered rebound, or a mistake on defense.

To create turnovers is our defense's major objective. The better we do this, the wider our margin of victory. Yet we do not wish to gamble to such an extent that our opposition will achieve an offensive advantage.

1. *Center Jump*: We begin our quest for turnovers with the center jump and the last possession in each quarter. We have set offensive and defensive techniques to gain control of this center jump four times each game. We also try to time it each quarter so that we take the last shot. This will give us four possessions more than our opposition, a potential of twelve points. Most games are won or lost by less margins.

2. *Held Balls*: There are two ways, one individually and one by the team, to force a held ball situation. Forcing the held ball, however, is only the first step in the turnover. The next step would be recovering the ensuing tip.

Individually, we use Drill No. 58 to teach our offense to avoid the tie up and our defense to force the jump ball.

Drill No. 58

Procedure

1. Line team up with one offensive and two defensive men in each group.
2. Give offensive men a ball. The offensive men have lost their dribble. They must learn to pivot, keeping the ball away from the two defenders.
3. The two defenders try to get one or two hands on the ball, trying to force a held ball situation without fouling.
4. Let each offensive man have the ball for 30 seconds. Total time of drill: one and one half minutes.

Objectives

1. To teach offensive men proper pivoting to protect ball.
2. To teach defenders proper techniques of gaining a held ball without fouling.

There are certain mechanics which will enable the defensive players to create more held ball situations. If the defender can get only one hand on the ball, he should move his body toward the ball, keeping his hand on the ball by sheer hustle.

Do not try a quick one-handed pull: rarely is one hand stronger than the two hands used by the opponent. In pulling at the ball, the defender will simply force himself to slide off the ball. He should be content to let the referee whistle a jump ball, taking his chances on a tip recovery.

If the defender can get two hands on the ball, he should immediately begin a steady pull and then suddenly jerk down. The moment the defensive man feels his opponent giving, the defender should use his body as a lever to pry the ball loose. If the defense is lucky, it will have the ball; if not, the least it should have is a held ball. This situation can occur many times during a game if the defenders are alert. How many times has the reader seen a big center rebound and bring a ball down around his midsection only to have a pint size guard take the ball away or tie up the center? The situation occurs often, and many times the center will lower the ball but no defender will try for the tie up. Constant training will get the defenders many of these held balls.

Teamwise we use Drill No. 59 (Diagram 6-1) to teach our defense to use the rules to force a held ball situation.

Drill No. 59

Procedure

1. Line up five men on offense with five defenders.
2. We allow 1 to dribble until X1 forces him to stop. We sometimes allow double-teaming help to stop the dribble. Then the double-teamer must hustle back to his man.
3. After the dribble has been stopped, all defenders contest the passing lanes to their man, forcing the held ball after five seconds.
4. We constantly remind the team of this during all five-on-five scrimmages.

Objectives

1. To teach 1 to dribble under pressure.
2. To teach X1 to halt the dribble; to teach double-teaming to stop the dribble, yet recovery to his own man to deny a return pass.

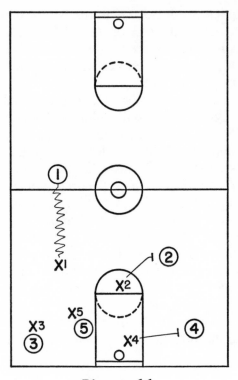

Diagram 6-1

3.   To teach coverage of the passing lanes so we can force the held ball.
4.   To teach 1 to pass under pressure.

The rule states that no player may dribble for five seconds or hold the ball for five seconds. We start with the first one-on-one drill the first day of practice constantly reminding our offensive players that they must perform their fakes and moves within five seconds. Our defense tries to make them dribble for six seconds. However, if the offense stops his dribble, we try to cover the receivers with pressure, hoping that the passer cannot get rid of the ball within five seconds. According to our defensive rules, our strong side men are already pressuring their passing lanes. That leaves only our weakside men who are trained from the first day of practice to get to their men and stay between them and the ball. The defender on the ball should yell and keep his arms moving up and down. He should not reach in for the steal because that would allow the passer better vision to the passing lanes.

Held balls occur more times during a game than a coach suspects. If the coach has trained his defenders well, this situation offers a golden opportunity to create turnovers.

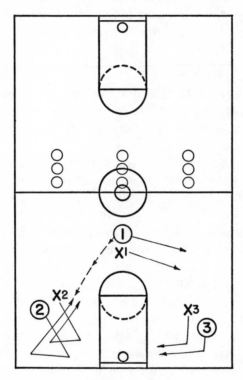

Diagram 6-2

Drill No. 60

Procedure

1. Line up three players on offense and three players on defense—rotate from offense to defense to end of line.
2. Passes must be thrown: absolutely no dribbling
3. X1, X2, and X3 try to prevent pass completions.
4. The drill is run until a lay-up occurs or a stolen pass results.

Objectives

1. To teach passing under extreme pressure.
2. To teach sealing off the passing lanes.
3. To teach aggressive coverage.
4. To teach player to receive pass going at full speed yet keep his balance and not walk.
5. To teach the passer to lead the receiver and to teach the passer to throw the pass on the side away from the defender.

We teach Drill No. 60 (Diagram 6-2) on the full court level as well as for half court defense. It is designed not only to intercept passes but to create the held ball situation. It also teaches proper body coverage on a cutter, staying between the cutter and the ball.

3. *Charging:* We are always trying to draw the charge. We feel this is as demoralizing to our opponent's offense as our fast break is to their defense. Almost all of our drills are designed to draw the charge, and we try to achieve this through the methods described in Chapter 3. Sometimes the offensive player will stop short of a charge but perpetrate a violation.

4. *Violations:* There are all kinds of violations of the rules. Walking or palming the ball occurs frequently when the defense offers pressure.

We try to create some violations. For example, we will attempt to legally hold a cutter in the three second lane. To do this we have our center step out in front of the cutter in the lane—to continue the cutter must charge, and if he stops and tries to go around the defensive center, we reverse pivot in front of the cutter. If he tries to go back out on the side from which he entered, his defender will reverse pivot in front of him. Usually three seconds will occur before the cutter can get out. We do this infrequently because it can result in an easy basket, but it should be good once or twice a game. Imaginative coaches can dream up other methods of forcing the violations. Violations are the greatest cause of turnovers.

5. *Intercepting Passes:* We consider every pass a loose ball until it is in the possession of the player who receives it. This does not mean that we will try to intercept every pass, but

we do have plans to intercept as many as feasible. We full court press with the intention of intercepting many passes, and we tell our half court zone men to intercept as many as possible. And in Chapter 8 we offer many of the stunts we use to try to intercept passes.

Double-teaming and shooting the gap is probably the best known way of intercepting passes. We also use this and we teach it by Drills No. 61 (Diagram 6-3) and 62 (Diagram 6-4).

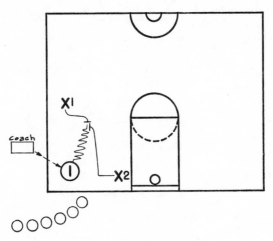

Diagram 6-3

Drill No. 61

Procedure

1. Line players up in one line—rotate from 1 to X1 to X2 to end of line.
2. Coach passes to 1 to activate the drill.
3. 1 tries to break the double-team by dribbling.
4. X1 tries to contain 1 until X2 arrives for double-team.
5. 1 keeps dribble alive while X1 and X2 force him into the corner. We like 1 to keep dribbling because it causes X1 and X2 to force 1 into the corner. This eliminates reaching in to steal the dribble while double-teaming, a cardinal defensive sin.

Objectives

1. To teach offensive dribbler to avoid the double-team.
2. To teach how to double-team correctly.
3. To teach one defender how to contain and another how to double-team. The container is to prevent vertical advancement; the double-teamer is to eliminate horizontal movement.

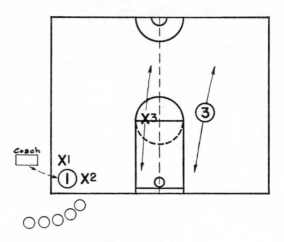

Diagram 6-4

Drill No. 62: Shoot the Gap Drill

Procedure

1. Line players in one line—rotate from 1 to X1 to X2 to 3 to X3 to end of line.
2. Coach passes to 1 to activate the drill.
3. 1 does not have a dribble or the drill at this stage can be run like Drill No. 61 with X1 and X2 stopping the dribble.
4. X1 and X2 double-team 1.
5. X3 must stay in interception distance of 3, but not up against him.
6. 3 can move up and down the court but does not come across a half court imaginary line (dotted).

7. After the double-team, 1 tries to pass to 3 and X3 tries to intercept. 1 must not lob pass.

Objectives

1. To teach defender how to shoot the gap and steal a pass.
2. To teach 1 how to pass under double-team pressure.
3. To teach double-teamers proper method of forcing a bad pass to help X3 pick off the pass.
4. To teach X3 perfect position to shoot the gap for a steal.

Our defense encourages the man who is under double-team pressure to throw either a lob or a bounce pass. We try almost always to double team off the dribble. That way we eliminate one of the moves of the offense, and we have in mind to dictate to the offense the use of two definite passes: the bounce and the lob.

In order to force these two passes, we use a dictating technique. We approach the offensive man with caution, never allowing him a chance to split us with the dribble. Once the offensive man has lost his dribble, we assume a tight, narrow base. The narrow base is important; it encourages the bounce pass. Our inside feet are perpendicular to each other. Our outside arms are high, and our inside arms are located at the knee and at the shoulder. Our arms are in constant motion.

Because of the positioning of our feet and our inside arms, it is almost impossible for the offensive man to step through the area between us. He will make a bounce pass around us, or he will throw a lob pass over us.

The offensive man could leave his feet. If he does, we leave ours. The offensive man cannot come down with the ball without walking. We try to deflect a level pass, forcing the lob. We never reach in to try for the steal. This is the most useless foul in basketball. It only allows the offense an easy way out of the advantage gained by the defense. Drills No. 61 and 62 help us perfect these techniques.

There are three passing lanes: to the left, center, and right. There should be an interceptor near each lane regardless of the defense being used. This interceptor should shield himself from the view of the passer, and he should only be three to five feet off a straight line between the receiver and the passer. The distance can be greater when quicker men are employed. The interceptor should have his weight forward and be on the balls of his feet in a coil position ready to spring forward much as a cat springs toward his prey. If the interceptor cannot get to the ball to intercept or deflect it, he must cover the receiver very tight for a second or so. This prevents another penetrating pass before the defense recovers sufficiently to double-team again. This tight pressure also causes some walking violations; or at the least, it will cause a momentary pause by the new receiver, giving the other defenders enough time to recover.

Mastery of the above techniques is demanded during early season drills so that the players are ready to use them when we begin teaching full court man-to-man and zone pressure defenses.

6. *Forcing Free Balls and Recovering Them:* We list this as a sixth method of turnover primarily because we do not intercept all passes; we deflect some. We have many drills, as the reader has seen in other chapters, where the ball is deflected, and we have players going for the recovery. This is what we call the hustling battle within the game itself, and we try to win that battle.

7. *Forcing Bad Shots:* All our stances and our defensive efforts go first to preventing the offense from getting off the shot. The mathematical principle of basketball indicates that the longer the offensive team holds the ball, the greater their probability of error. With every pass and every dribble, this probability increases. However, should the offense get off the shot, we try to make it a bad shot. Once the shot is in the air, it is a free ball; and we try to tilt the odds in favor of our recovering it. This leads into the third primary method of getting control of the ball: defensive and offensive rebounding. In this book, we only concern ourselves with defensive rebounding.

REBOUNDING

Most coaches agree that the team that controls the rebounding controls the game. This is not always true, but the mathematics of basketball usually substantiates it. There is an average of 80 to 85 "loose balls" coming off the boards every game. The easiest method of controlling the game is to control these "loose balls."

Height alone will not secure these rebounds; positioning will. Our tallest player in a recent season was a 6' 1" guard playing center, yet we managed to out-rebound our taller opposition (39.6 to 38.1). That is the importance of positioning.

Defensive rebounding must be stressed daily until it becomes habitual. If we are to play great defense, we must not allow the second shot. Boxing-out is the problem; one shot per possession is the principle. And remember it is much easier to box-out while playing an aggressive man-to-man defense than it is while playing a passive zone.

If we choose to play an aggressive or passive zone, we assign a rebound triangle. But for our man-to-man defensive rebounding efforts, we use four methods of obtaining box-out positioning: reverse pivots, front pivots, facing, and cross blockouts.

To supplement our defensive rebounding we use a count system. In each of the rebounding box-out techniques, the defender should be watching his opponent until the last possible second. It is, therefore, necessary to know when to turn to face the basket. We count 1,001, 1,002, etc. to determine when to turn. A shot from 5' to 10' has a 1,001 count, 10' to to 15' has 1,002 count, 15' to 20' has 1,003 count, and from 20' out, 1,004 and estimate. If our offensive man has not moved during the needed count, we turn immediately to the basket, sight the ball, and jump for the rebound.

However, if the offensive man fakes and tries to roll for an offensive rebound, we must box him out in order to safely secure inside or box-out position. The position our man is in from the basket and his quickness in comparsion to our quickness determine the box-out technique we will use. It only takes a moment to teach each method; and, when mastered, it virtually assures the defender of the rebound, a must for effective defensive play.

Reverse pivots are used in close to the basket. That is the area where the defender can take advantage of its strengths and lose nothing to its weaknesses. Reverse pivots are slower to execute, and easier to succumb to offensive fakes than the front pivots. The reason for this weakness is simple: the defender has to take his eyes off the offensive rebounder earlier than under other methods, and he must pivot on the first fake. Consequently the defensive rebounder can lose position on a fake right go left move. But reverse pivots will enable the defender to get his eyes on the rebound quicker.

Therefore, the reader can see the advantage of using reverse pivots near the basket. There is a great need to face the rebound quickly (1,001 count), and there is not enough area for the offensive rebounder to use his fakes effectively, nor does he have enough time.

Diagram 6-5

To use the reverse pivot, the defender must be acquainted with its mechanics. Diagram 6-5 shows the proper technique. As the offensive man goes right, the defensive man's reverse pivot should be on his left foot, swinging his right foot around between himself and the basket in such a way that the defensive man's back is always to the offensive man.

Front pivots are used from ten feet out because this is adjusting to the advantages of the front pivot and losing nothing to its disadvantages. From that distance, there is no need to see the ricochet of the rebound quickly; but there is a great need to keep the eyes on the offensive rebounder longer because the offensive man has a greater area in which to fake. The front pivot allows this. The mechanics are illustrated in Diagram 6-6.

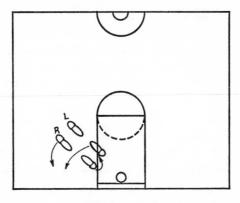

Diagram 6-6

Diagram 6-6 shows the offense going right after he is through faking. It also shows the front pivot executed by the defender. The pivot is again on the left foot, but this time the defensive rebounder swings his right foot around in front of himself, between himself and the offense.

Although both of these methods are excellent, and both can be used to their fullest advantage by applying the above strategy, there are those great offensive rebounders who defy box-outs because of their extreme quickness and natural tack of being in the right place at the right time. To halt these exceptional rebounders, we resort to a move we call "facing." The defender we assign to this offensive rebounder is told not to worry about securing the rebound. His sole job is to always face his opponent, except when he goes inside where we reverse pivot, never allowing the offensive man to get around the defensive man. This helps eliminate the advantages of this exceptional offensive rebounder.

Another method we have to use is the cross blockout because occasionally we get caught playing in front of an offensive inside man when a shot is taken. In this case, if the man who is being fronted is a good rebounder, we allow the opposite side forward to come over and box-out the center. Then the defensive center crosses over to box-out the offensive forward, or we drop an outside guard to box-out the offensive forward.

We also have to worry about weakside box-outs. This happens frequently during a game. These weakside men go out to pick up their offensive men while counting. They race toward the offensive man's inside, then as the offense starts outside, we pivot (reverse or front whichever is applicable) outside and go for the rebound. Going out to meet the offside forward keeps us from getting caught too close to the basket.

Boxing-out does not always secure excellent floor position. It only gives the defender the inside. It is up to the defense to pressure his man sufficiently so that the defender will always have an excellent strategic area of the court.

After obtaining inside position and a good place on the court (as far away from the basket as possible), the defender should take up as much room as possible. He should have a good wide base with his elbows and trunk out. He should be in a coil position, ready to spring upward and forward toward the hoop. This take off leap prevents the offensive man from keeping body contact with the defensive rebounder, eliminating the possible tie-up on a high rebound.

The defender's next job is to secure the loose ball. To do this, he should jump as high as he can and the jump should be forward, toward the rebound. He should do this in a spread-eagle movement. When he grabs the ball, it should be with two hands, and it should be snapped out of the air. The ball should never be tipped around while on the defensive end of the court.

Now that the defender has secured the rebound, he must be able to protect it. He should land in the spread-eagle position, ready to pivot on either foot. If he is a big man, he should bring the ball to the area around his chin with his elbows out and moving. If he is a small guard, he should bring the ball real low and keep it moving. He is now on offense.

We use many drills to teach these rebounding techniques. They each must be used frequently in order to establish the habit of positioning. Defensive rebounding cannot be overemphasized.

Drill No. 63

Procedure

1.   Line players up in 3 lines as shown—rotate from offense to defense to end of line.

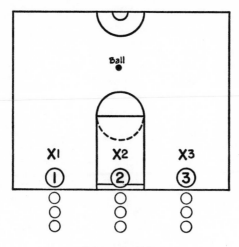

Diagram 6-7

2. Place ball near midcourt.
3. Offense may use any fake they wish.
4. Defender must use box-out technique coach wishes—it is always predetermined.
5. Defenders keep contact as long as legally possible.
6. 1, 2, and 3 try to get to the basketball.
7. If the school owns a McCall's Rebounder, it is best to put the ball on the arm of the Rebounder and drill on the snap recovery with both hands.

Objectives

1. To teach offensive rebounding.
2. To teach defensive box-out techniques (special emphasis is always placed on this phase of rebounding).
3. To teach proper methods of recovering the rebound.

Drill No. 63 should be used with special emphasis on all the box-out techniques. Master the reverse and front pivot techniques first. Occasionally a slower man will get a much quicker and more experienced one. When this happens, let him use the facing method and watch how easily the offensive rebounder is stopped.

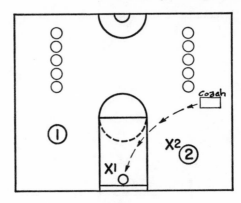

Diagram 6-8

Drill No. 64

Procedure

1. Line players up as shown—rotate from offense to defense to end of other line.
2. X1 can be instructed to box-out 1, teaching our weakside rebounding theory; X2 would have to use a reverse pivot (remember: we have one foot behind the offensive post man).
3. X1 and X2 can be instructed to cross blockout, teaching our cross blockout techniques.

Objectives

1. To teach offensive rebounding from weakside and side post.
2. To teach defensive rebounding on weakside, cross blockouts, and reverse pivoting box-outs.

Drill No. 65

Procedure

1. Line players up as shown—rotate from offense to defense to end of line.
2. Coach moves about and shoots. The three defenders use box-out techniques that the coach wants.
3. The count method is employed and the rebound is retrieved.

4. The rebounders may be moved in and out so as to change the distance from the basket.
5. The coach could require the defenders to sluff off the ball the correct distance by use of our defensive principles.
6. The coach can move after shooting, forcing the defensive rebounders to re-locate him for an outlet pass on fast break.

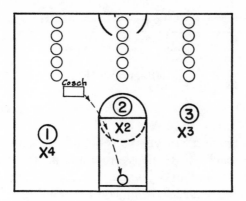

Diagram 6-9

Objectives

1. To teach rebounding techniques (offensive and defensive).
2. To teach recovery techniques.
3. To teach protection of the rebound.
4. To teach outlet passing for fast break.

Drill No. 66

Procedure

1. Line five offensive players up against five defensive players.
2. 1, 2, and 3 pass ball around with proper sluffs by the defense until one of them shoots.
3. X4 and X5 practice their appropriate sags, and when shots are taken, the proper box-out techniques are employed.

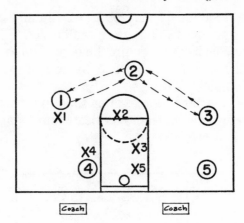

Diagram 6-10

Objectives

1.   To teach all offensive rebounding techniques.
2.   To teach all defensive rebounding techniques.
3.   To teach team defensive sags and rebounding: weak-side as well as strongside rebounding.

Drill No. 64 (Diagram 6-8) teaches the next two box-out techniques, and it must be used frequently. After mastering these five techniques, go to Drill No. 65 (Diagram 6-9) and require any box-out method. For variety the coach may let one line use one technique and another line another technique. He may change the distance the rebounders are from the basket. Drill No. 66 (Diagram 6-10) concludes the drill we use on defensive rebounding. It is a team rebounding drill which brings into play all the defensive rebounding techniques and methods.

Every player must box-out his man on every shot. If one offensive man gets through, the other four men will have boxed-out in vain. It truly requires a team effort.

SEVEN

Breaking Down
and Defensing
Pattern Basketball

In this chapter, the reader will notice that the defense of each situation is only an application and an amplification of the principles of our pressure defense (Chapter 2).

Most of the situations described in this chapter have also been covered fundamentally in Chapters 3, 4, and 5.

There is no intent for this chapter to be taught as a unit nor are drills offered. This information is given so that the reader can understand how our fundamentals and principles check the part plays of our opposition's offense. We scout our opponents and then break their offense into the part plays described in this chapter. We then drill on the defense of those part plays. By season's end, even the most inexperienced player should know how to defense the most complicated of offenses.

Coaches differ in offensive philosophy: some like to emphasize one man plays, others stress two or three man plays. It is up to the defensive coach to observe the opponent's offensive philosophy, and then to stress the defense of the part plays that reflects the opposition's offensive emphasis.

The reader should store in a file the knowledge gained from a study of the opposition coach. He will find that the opposing coach will not readily change his offensive philosophy. The file can be used from year to year. The reader should not restrict his knowledge to memory; he should reduce it to writing and re-use the information annually.

On many part plays, we have several methods of covering the options. This is where defensive strategy plays an important part. We adopt the method that we think will hurt our opponents the most. Also, as our talent changes, we change to take advantage of it.

HOW A PATTERN DESTROYS OFFENSE
AND HELPS DEFENSE

Patterns, when adhered to regimentally, make robots out of offensive basketball players. When the robot is unplugged, he stops and his work remains undone. When a team is forced out of its patterns, it stops and chaos results.

Patterns work best against the non-thinking, rigidly controlled defense. Patterns against weak non-pressure ball clubs will work like the finest clock ever made. But unless the offensive coach permits some free-styling options, allowing his team to read the defense and react, his team will not likely win the ultimate championship. His offense will be stopped by the third running unless he has been scouted, and then it might be stopped on the first running. Pattern teams are more easily scouted, more easily defensed, more easily defeated.

A team cannot learn enough patterns to be successful against a good defense. The defense will move with the offense and run the offensive patterns. If taught to stay with the pattern, instead of reacting to defensive dictated options, the offense will fold.

Pattern offenses require time to perfect, taking away precious practice time which could be used to teach basketball fundamentals.

HOW A PATTERN HELPS OFFENSE
AND HURTS DEFENSE

Free-styling does not have the crisp timing of a patterned

offense, weakening the execution of the part plays from which both styles are made. Free-styling usually leads to the weakside offensive players not moving. In pattern-style ball, the offside movement is pre-planned and must be carried out to keep the pattern continuous. Free-styling usually leads to more dribbling and domination of the game by one or two better players. Team offensive play is far superior to individual play.

Defensing becomes easy if the offense is standing. The three or so zone men can easily clog up such a free-style offense.

If the pattern players are patient, even the best trained defenders will make a mistake. Patterns can create unity out of a group of inexperienced players.

THE COMPLETE PATTERN TEAM CAN BE SHUT OUT

Our dream, the shut out, may someday be accomplished, maybe not by us but by someone. It will come at the expense of the rigidly controlled patterned offense.

A few years ago we thoroughly scouted a rigidly controlled team. At the half, they had not scored a field goal and we led 36-3. In our return match with that team, they discarded their controlled game, caught us off guard, and defeated us 88-86.

Also, a few years ago we played a team that was a preseason favorite to win its district. They ran isolations and two man plays. While these part plays occurred, the other three players remained immobile. Our zone men took over and at half we led 58-12.

We were fortunate enough one year to meet two teams in a row in a post season tournament that ran patterned offenses without proper options. We held them without a field goal for 28 minutes 16 seconds consecutively: the last half of one game, the first half of the next. During that span, we scored 92 points. There was no holding of the ball, just good, aggressive, pressure defense, properly executed.

MOST COACHES BREAK THEIR OFFENSES INTO DRILLS

Most coaches teach their offense by drills. The wise ones teach only the drills that are in their offense. We believe in defensing them in the same way. We break down their offense into part plays; then we defense each of those part plays. We will break down the famous offenses of basketball into part plays at the end of this chapter to show details of our team defensive techniques.

ALL TEAM OFFENSES HAVE
THE SAME FUNDAMENTALS

Basketball offenses are varied in name only. There are the Auburn Shuffle, the Weave, the 1-3-1, the Wheel, the Five Moving Pivots and many, many more.

Offensive minded coaches can choose from these tried and successful patterns. They can free-lance, use variations of the above patterns, or with imagination dream up their own.

Although some coaches would say each pattern is different, they would admit that all of them have identical elements. They just perform these recurring maneuvers at different phases or at different times in their patterns. We have isolated these identical elements, and we have worked out sound defenses against each one, basing these defenses on our defensive fundamentals (Chapter 3, 4, and 5) and our pressure principles (Chapter 2).

All teams, except those that isolate completely, have some sort of patterns built around screens that they practice daily. If we can cancel out the effectiveness of these screens, we can force our opponents to operate virtually without practice. This leads to total chaos, and their chaotic condition leads to our victory.

We offer one major don't: don't drill on this chapter until the fundamentals have been mastered. Otherwise, the athletes will respond as robots instead of thinking defensively; and if this happens, when something new appears in a game, the defense will collapse.

But if the defense has mastered the first six chapters, if the coaches have done a good job scouting the opponents, and if each part play has been broken down as in this chapter, the resistance will have minimized the results of any offense.

1. *Stopping the Give and Go:* In our terminology, the give and go is an offensive pass and an inside cut (between the ball and his defender) for a return pass. This move is very effective against pressure defenses, and it usually results in a lay-up.

We defense the give and go by our principle of a step in and toward every pass. This, as we said before, is a long jump step. Our peripheral vision enables us to see our offensive man coming, and we overplay our offensive man until he cuts behind us or charges over us. The offense has other options: he can cut behind the man he passed to but we call this the go behind; or the offense can cut behind his own defender, and we call that the backdoor cut.

The only way for the give and go move to be successful against our pressure defense is for the passer's defender to cheat a glance without stepping toward the receiver. In that case, the offensive passer can easily cut between his defender and the ball for an uncontested pass. This is a defensive mistake that can be eliminated by mastering the basic principle: step in and toward every pass.

2. *Defensing the Backdoor Cut:* The backdoor cut (along with the give and go) is the most widely used of the four basic cuts. The other two individual cuts are the middle cut and the go behind.

The backdoor is extremely successful against the defender who glances toward the passer or against the defensive man who has not learned to help out, yet recover on his own man. Both of these defensive mistakes are eliminated in our fundamental drills.

This offensive pattern starts with a pass followed by a cut. The object of the cut is to go behind the cutter's defender, receiving a pass for the lay-up (Diagram 7-1). It is not mandatory for the backdoor cutter to be the initial passer.

In Diagram 7-1, if X1 has properly positioned himself and has not glanced toward 2 but kept good peripheral vision, then 2 would have to complete a pass through two men to be successful. Or 2 could throw a lob pass which is most difficult to complete, and if not perfectly thrown, easily intercepted by X1.

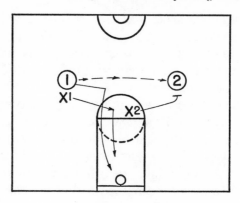

Diagram 7-1

A real good pattern for the backdoor is shown by Diagram 7-5 in the section on defensing the fake split. The proper coverage for this backdoor cut by 1 is for X4 to cut 4 toward the congestion (to the right). That would leave X1 to cover 1 as we regularly cover the backdoor cutter. X2, X3, and X5 should be saying "help" to let X4 know which way to cut 4. Remember that X4 would deny a pass to 4 below the free throw line, forcing the play to originate high, helping the defense contain the backdoor play.

3. *Defensing the Middle Cut:* To offensively execute the middle cut, in our definition of terms, there need not be a pass and a cut, just the cut. The idea is to cut the same as in the give and go (between the ball and the defender).

The defense of this is simple: sag to the proper position, never allowing the offensive man to cut between the defender and the ball, forcing the offense to go backdoor or to go behind the man with the ball.

This play is rarely effective against an alert defense. It is included here so as not to leave any stones unturned in our quest for the impossible dream: the shut out.

4. *Defensing the Go Behind:* We define the go behind as a pass then a cut behind the receiver. It is used to set up a screen shot over the receiver or for a driving lay-up on a hand off (flip) pass. It is also used to set up the blast which will be discussed later.

It can be set up by a pass to an outside man and go behind

him or to an inside man and blast. Both moves are extremely effective unless properly defensed. The outside pass is more effective at setting up the next play, not at scoring itself. The outside pass will be discussed in this section; the inside pass will be discussed in the section on defensing the blast.

The primary responsibility of defensing the outside maneuver belongs to the defender on the receiver. If he is a guard, he is outside the key (left side illustration in Diagram

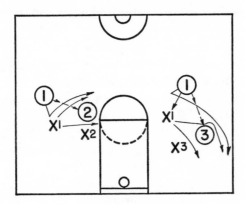

Diagram 7-2

7-2). X2 covers 2 and X1 has the option of going over the top to prevent his man from getting the ball back or sliding through. The option belongs to X1, and X2 must be ever alert to opening and letting X1 slide through. We do not worry about the guard shooting from that distance: he cannot score consistently from there. By opening, it keeps X1 on 1, X2 on 2, and it prevents 2 from shooting because X1 is near him.

On the right side of the illustration, X3 should have denied the pass to 3 until he is out of normal scoring range. Then we proceed with X1 and X3 cooperating in the same manner as X1 and X2.

In both options, the offense has little chance of scoring. It is the inside blast that can be effective. We include the blast under another category because it does not require a pass and a cut. However, the pass and go behind sets up the next offensive maneuver, so it is best to fight over the top not allowing the cutter to receive the ball. An aggressive defender, especially one pre-warned by scouting reports, can stop this return pass, thereby eliminating the ensuing pattern.

Many times we will double-team the cutter immediately after the hand-off pass. We then shoot the gap, trying for an interception should the ball be passed back to the initial screener.

5. *Defensing the Screen and Roll:* The screen and roll can occur on the strong side or on the weak side. It is a positive screen, with the screener moving within inches of the person being screened, followed by a roll to the basket by the screener.

When this screen and roll occurs on the weakside, we call it an offside screen (see later section this chapter). When the screen occurs involving the ball, we begin our defense with the aggressive jump switch (see Chapter 3). However, we try to avoid switching by fighting over the top and by preventing the screener easy access to the man he intends to screen.

But if the maneuver is successful, the man being screened must place his forearm against the screener with considerable pressure. The screener's defender must call "watch screen" to let his teammate know the screen is coming. The screener's defender then calls "switch" as he jumps in front of the dribbler. As the screener rolls, the pressure of the forearm will cause the defender who was screened to open to the ball, creating perfect coverage on the roll.

Most of the time the roller will be watching the dribbler for a return pass. This permits our zone men (weakside) to get in position to draw the charge. The weakside is also responsible for the lob pass because the man being screened hustles to get position between the roller and the ball.

The defender who executes the jump switch must be careful that the dribbler does not change direction for an advantage. Constant drilling on this much used offensive maneuver will alert the defenders to all possibilities, and will facilitate their coverage, forfeiting the advantage of the screen and roll.

Sometimes we double-team the screener, especially if it is a reasonable distance from the basket. Shooting the gap between the dribbler and the roller sometimes results in a stolen pass. The double-team discourages two offensive men from congregating with the ball, thereby discouraging the screen and roll.

6. *Defensing the Blind Pick:* The blind pick occurs whenever an offensive post or corner man sets a screen for a dribbling guard. Its offensive reasoning is deadly: the offense wants to get the jump shot over the pick, or the offense wants to get the smaller guard mismatched on the taller corner or post man. The lethal blind pick can also be executed by a forward and center cooperating.

To defense this offensive team maneuver we use the center hedging theory unless the offense is outside shooting range. In that case, we let the picking defender open and allow the dribbling defender to slide through.

We begin by demanding that the inside defender use the word "pick." This informs the defender on the ball where a pick possibility exists, and it tells the defensive guard where help is. The defensive guard is always instructed to cut his man into the center, cutting down the passing angle in case of a screen and roll.

The defensive center must always be on the side of his man where the ball is. This enables the defense to use the hedging move which forces the offense to charge, to cut to the outside, to reverse directions, or to pick up the ball. None of those four cases are attacking moves. A review of the center hedging section in Chapter 5 will show how our coverage is effective.

No matter how hard we try, sometimes this offensive maneuver is successful. The only time that can occur is when the inside defensive man has made a mistake. And when the maneuver is successful we cover it as a screen and roll move.

Here again we may double-team to disrupt the rhythm of the pattern, and we may shoot the gap on the pass to the picker on his roll. Not only can we steal some passes, but we can discourage the play by double-teaming the ball and two attackers. Our weakside men can also draw the charge on the roll.

7. *Defensing the Inside Screen:* In our nomenclature, an inside screen means a pass and then go screen for the receiver. It is designed to get the jumper over the screen, the drive by the screen, or a pass back to the screener on a roll.

We begin our defense of this option by forcing the receiver as high as possible before he can get the pass. In this way we hope to avoid the high percentage shot over the screen.

We prevent the drive around the screen by jump switching, and we cover the roll the same as under the section on defensing the screen and roll.

Double-team pressure will work as these two offensive men come together, and sometimes stunting or shooting the gap will result in interceptions. Double-teaming will, after a few minutes, disrupt offensive timing and discourage the congregation of two attackers and the ball. That, in itself, will eliminate this offensive option.

8. *Defensing the Dribbling Screens:* The weave offense is an example of the dribbling screens. Their purpose: to create a jump shot over the screen or a driving lay-up going around the screen.

The dribbling screen is a highly effective method of scoring, but it has a weakness. And this weakness is what the defense should exploit. While the offensive man is dribbling, he cannot be concentrating on screening. Protection of the ball is his primary concern; screening is secondary, leaving the cutter to take the dip and set up his own screen.

In defensing this patterned option, we begin by having the defender on the cutter sag the required step on and toward the ball. With proper peripheral vision, this defender should be able to see the screen coming and to fight over the top by beating his man to a favorable offensive spot. That would leave one-on-one coverage on the dribbler.

If the offense is outside 20 feet, we do not fear the jumper over the screen, so we open up and slide through with the man on the ball opening.

Should it be a perfectly executed screen, we would jump switch, going into our coverage of a screen and a roll.

Double-teaming on the dribbling screen is also good. In fact, we double-team a lot on this pattern to discourage its use. Many times the defensive team will get an offensive team to shy from putting the ball and two offensive men together.

On occasions we will overplay a dribbler going to set a

screen, especially if they have been extremely successful. This way we can force the screener away from a screen he would like to set.

9. *Defensing the Screen and Go Behind:* This complex option consists of two simple, two-man plays: the inside screen which occurs first, where 1 screens for 2, but instead of rolling, 1 comes back over the top of 2 for a jump shot (Diagram 7-3).

It has all the shot options of the inside screen pattern plus all the options of the dribbling screen and roll. And we cover it in the same manner: first, as we would cover the inside screen

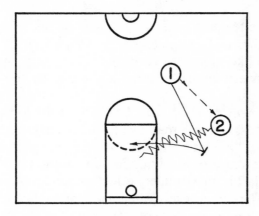

Diagram 7-3

(screen and roll if it is successful); second, as we would cover the dribbling screens.

The defense can also double-team anywhere the ball and two men cross. That is an extremely effective method of stopping this part-play. The defenders can pick either of two spots.

10. *Don't Let Them Shoot Over a Screen:* We have a motto: if the defender's man shoots over him, there is no help. This is a two edge sword: not only is there no defensive help, but there is no help for the defensive man. We bench the defender who is consistently tardy with his coverage of the shot over the screen.

If the defender is alert, he should not have any trouble

fighting over the top. And if the defense fights over the top, there can be no shot over the screen.

We always try to help the man who has to fight over the top. Hedging is the most used method of help; some other methods of helping have been explained in this and preceding chapters.

Sometimes screens are successful. When they are effective and we have to switch, we jump switch. This prevents the nonpressured jump shot.

It is much more effective to fight over the top, but, secondarily, we jump switch. Each defensive solution should be followed by a secondary solution should the first be unsuccessful.

Double-teaming when two offensive men and the ball come together will completely erase any advantage gained by teams who like to shoot over screens. Stunting and shooting the gap between the ball handler and the roller could result in turnovers.

11. *Defensing the Blast:* The blast is the term we use to indicate a pass to a big man inside and a small man, guard or forward, breaking off him. It results in a high percentage jump shot for the guard or a driving lay-up for the inside man.

The blast is an extremely effective pattern when executed properly. The center receives the ball, and as the guard cuts by him, pivots on his inside foot, screening the guard's defender with his back. Then the center decides: hand off to 1 if screen is successful and no switch; drive if there is a switch (Diagram 7-4).

We begin our defense by refusing to let 5 receive the ball. Should 5 receive the ball, X5 must play him head-on, very tight, preventing 5 from stepping forward even one inch. This prevents 5 from pivoting and setting the near perfect screen for 1, and it also gives X1 a better chance to fight over the top.

X5 should have let X1 know that there was a pivot man by using the word "post." Also, X1, upon seeing the pass, steps in and toward the pass, and if X1 even suspects the blast, he edges toward 5 so that he can more easily fight over the top.

Not only is this the best coverage, it is the only coverage unless the offense makes a mistake. If the guard X1 slides through, 1 shoots a high percentage jump shot; if we switch, 5

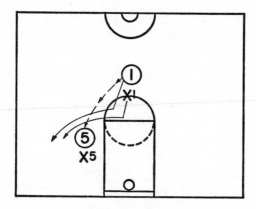

Diagram 7-4

drives for the easy lay-up.

Despite two offensive men converging where the ball is, it is not advisable to double-team the blast. First, the man with the ball is the big man, and an easy pass out to the guard is a 12' to 15' jump shot. Secondly, the action is too close to the bucket to enable good stunting and good recovery.

12. *Defensing the Split Off the Post:* This is one of the oldest team maneuvers in basketball, and without proper defense it is highly effective. It is designed to produce the screened jump shot or the lay-up for the cutters; it also can produce hooks, drives, or jumpers for the post men. This can be a cooperative effort between the two guards and a pivot man or between a guard, forward, and a side post man.

As the reader can recall from Chapter 5, we defense the post man in a manner that prevents him from getting the pass. If it is a two guard front, we also have help from the weakside guard; if it is a one guard front, help comes from the guard sluff and from the wings. So we begin our defense of the split by denying the pass to the pivot.

Once the post man does receive the pass, the two outside defenders must pressure their men outside. They must not drop too deeply off their men, and they must not switch. Their drop should be in toward the center. To drop outside off their men allows an inside cut by the offense, making it impossible to keep the cutter from receiving the ball for a driving lay-up. To switch permits the guards to both cut on the same side of the center (fake split), giving the second cutter through a wide open jump shot. So each defender is to cover his man with pressure, forcing the cutters to alter from their original path to a much wider one (farther away from the center). If this new path is only one step wider, it would permit the defenders to slide through, and it would permit them to fight over the top in case one of the cutters decides to fake a split and come back over the center's pick. This is in agreement with our principle of not permitting the horizontal or lateral pass within 25′ of the basket, as we are between our man and the ball (center).

Sometimes the first cutter will try to stop and set a screen for the second cutter. When this happens, the second guard must force his man above the pivot and the screener. If he is unsuccessful at this, the second cutter will be coming near the inside leg of the first cutter and our first cutter's defender should be right there to draw the charge. In case everything fails, which is highly unlikely, we have the other two defenders, those not involved in the play, sinking. It will not fail if the two guards will not sink behind the offensive pivot man.

The center should have already called out "post," alerting the outside defenders to the split possibility. Anytime a pass is successful inside, we drop toward the pass forcing the ball out, but we do this drop in such a way that we will not be picked by the man with the ball. In other words we try to force the backdoor cut instead of the inside cut off the split.

13. *Defensing the Fake Split:* This is a continuation of the splitting the post maneuver. This time, however, one of the offensive guards does not split but rather proceeds down the same side as the splitting guard.

To defense this maneuver, we continue our defensing of the actual split. As the reader recalls, our guards are next to the center just a step or two higher. When the first guard goes through, it is easy for the defender to follow his man, forcing the offense outside. When the second guard makes his maneuver, if it is down the same side, we already are between him and the ball, plus we have extra backdoor help: the defender on the first guard through. If it is a fake down one side, then an attempt to cut back over the top of the center for a jump shot, our defensive man must pressure the second guard as many steps outside as he can. This enables the defender to fight over the top and not allow the pass, preventing the shot over the screen.

The offense could clear out one side of the court, pass into a forward breaking up to high post, then fake a split by sending a guard backdoor (Diagram 7-5). This move has been covered in defensing the backdoor cut (this chapter).

14. *Defensing the Offside Screen:* This screen is set up away from the ball. Unlike its kindred, the rub-off (Auburn Shuffle is an example), this screen is set within inches of the

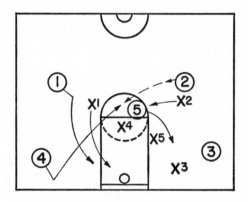

Diagram 7-5

man being screened. There is no maneuvering by the cutter to help the screener. The cutter merely breaks around the screen for a pass.

Defending this offensive maneuver is not difficult. Always remember to never play an attacker moving away from the ball tightly.

Diagram 7-6 shows how the weakside defender's sag enables good coverage. X1, with proper positioning, can easily see the screener, 5, coming. X1 moves in the direction of the ball should a pass be thrown, beating his man high in this case or low if the ball is below the cut. The only way 5 can screen X1 is by moving up and this is an illegal moving screen. Remember though, X1 must crash into 5 for this violation to be called.

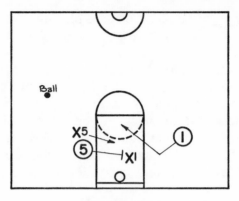

Diagram 7-6

Should the defender X1 not be concentrating and the screen be successful, X5 can use the hedging technique, slowing down 1 until X1 can fight around the screen and recover.

As a last resort, the two defenders can switch, a defensive maneuver that should never have to take place if everyone away from the ball is concentrating. Should 1 come racing recklessly around the screen, X5 can move in front of 1 drawing the charge, the defender's delight, one that, as the reader has noticed, we love to perform.

15. *Defensing the Pass and Screen Away:* The pass and screen away is exactly what the name implies—a player passes and goes away from the ball to set a screen. The man being screened, dips, then breaks over the screen for a pass and a potential score (Diagram 7-7).

This move is effective only when X1 is lulled asleep by his man cutting away from the ball. If X2 has properly sagged and is prepared, he should easily avoid the screen.

We cover this move the same as we covered the offside screen. If our defenders are alert, this option will not be successful.

16. *Defensing the Vertical Rub-off:* Rub-offs have become intergral parts of many offenses. The vertical rub-off (Diagram 7-8) is used by almost all teams using double post offenses.

The idea of the rub-off: an offensive man runs his man into a stationary screen (usually a blind pick, which cannot legally be set without giving the defender one full step). The

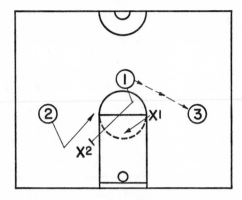

Diagram 7-7

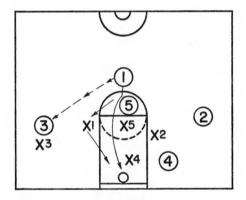

Diagram 7-8

rub-off is usually a pass followed by a semi give and go cut.

This offensive basic can be defended easily by applying our basic principle of stepping one step in and toward each pass. This puts our defender on the ball side of the screen and on the ball side of the cutter.

Another advantage for the defense: if the defensive center is alert and the offense uses this maneuver many times, the defensive center can easily draw the charge. The cutter is probably busy watching the pass receiver for a return pass. In Diagram 7-8, both X4 and X5 would have good opportunities for drawing the charge.

In Chapter 5 we discussed the possibilities of the center

and weakside men picking up many charging fouls. It really discourages an offensive team, especially those that are slaves to pattern movement.

17. *Defensing the Lateral Rub-off:* The lateral rub-off, shown in Diagram 7-9, is used by such offenses as the Shuffle, and it is used often by many imaginative coaches.

1 tries to rub his man off on 5. Good initial defensive positioning is required to defend against this often used offensive maneuver. We always force the cutter away from the ball,

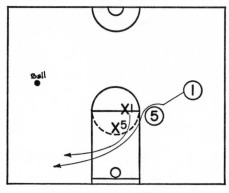

Diagram 7-9

staying between the ball and the cutter. So if the ball is high, X1 would slide over the top of 5; if the ball is low, X1 would sluff underneath 5. This would permit X1 to beat 1 to the spot of greatest advantage, which would change with each pass, and force 1 away from the ball.

An alert post man can easily draw some charges; and an alert coach can prompt his pivot defender to the possibilities. Draw the charge a few times and watch the opponents lose their poise. The result will be a wide-margin victory.

18. *Defensing the Multiple Screens:* The multiple (double and triple) screens are part of many offenses. They are designed to get a cutter open either behind the screen for a jump shot or cutting off the screen for a lay-up. Unfortunately, it takes long hours of practicing the pattern to get the necessary timing.

There are several ways the multiple screen can be set into

motion. For example, it can be set away from the ball, as in the Wheel. In that case the sag should enable our defender to get around the double or triple screen.

We prefer our defender to always go over the top. This usually forces his offensive man around the screen low (if not, we have him covered, being between him and the ball). This way we can always be sure of cutting hard to beat the cutter to a spot low. Besides, we always have the low man on the double or triple screen switch if necessary. We also have him hedge and slow down the cutter. The low defender is also in the perfect place to draw the charge. But, if we have to switch, each man slides down a man. Doing it this way also keeps us in inside rebounding position.

If the offense decides to pass the ball back around for a jump shot behind the screen, we have found it easier to pressure the passing lane, then pressure the shot by always going over the top. If we have to, we also switch down: let the low man take the cutter and the others switch down one man.

When the multiple screen involves the ball, we always try to recognize it coming. We pressure the outside men, allowing the defender on the man who is going to shoot to fight over the top. We try to prevent him from getting the ball much less the shot. The reader may wonder how we know that the double or triple screen is coming: scouting is the answer. There is no way for a free-lance team to run such a screen because their timing would never be efficient enough to be effective.

The multiple screen can be sprung as a susprise occasionally, but if the defenders are trained in fundamentals and good defensive thinking, they can adjust. Or if the defenders have mastered the technique of switching down one man, they will be sufficiently prepared to handle the multiple screen.

DEFENSING THE BASIC PATTERNS

Before beginning a discussion of full court and stunting defense, we should draw our half court regular defense together by stopping, on paper, the great offenses of basketball. By great offenses we do not mean a style of play but rather a system of patterns. And all patterns, regardless of how effective they originally are, have weaknesses. These weaknesses should be exploited.

1. *Isolations:* A lot of teams use patterns that end up in clearouts, and some ball clubs operate exclusively from one-on-one basketball. We defense these moves as explained in Chapter 1, using front foot to pivot foot stance before the dribble, and using parallel stance and the overplay after the dribble. We always force the ball to help, which is known by the defender on the ball when he hears "help" from his teammates. One-on-one basketball will not beat the good teams.

2. *The Wheel:* Diagrams 7-10, 7-11, and 7-12 show this famous continuity. The first action is calling the play: a pass from a guard into a forward. Our corner pressure defense should force the play high and outside, making it hard for 4 to

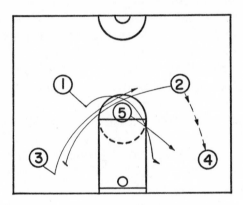

Diagram 7-10

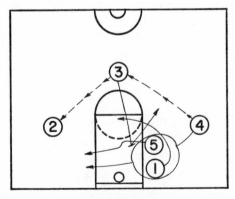

Diagram 7-11

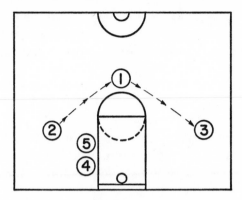

Diagram 7-12

pass inside or for 4 to take an effective jump shot. We like to encourage this forward to jump shoot, especially if he is a weak shooter. If the reader notices closely, both guards have gone down under the basket, leaving the floor unbalanced and vulnerable to a fast break. It also weakens the offensive rebounding with two guards in front court.

Our first job is to stop the pass to the guard, 1, on his cut. This is what we call the middle cut, and its defense is clearly outlined in this chapter. The next part play, the screen away from the ball, 3 screened for by 2, is also covered in this chapter. Defensing the above options ends the first phase of the attack.

We now begin the second phase of the defense, the continuity or turnover (Diagram 7-11). We sometimes shoot the gap on the pass to 3, but mostly we sink and cover 3 when he receives the pass. We do cover the pass to 2, a vertical penetrating pass, in an aggressive, pressure manner, using our fencing slide. Should 2 receive a pass, we want it out of good scoring range. This gives the offense a temporary clearout move, which we defense as an isolation. Forcing the reception outside not only prevents an immediate high percentage shot, but it also makes it difficult to complete the inside pass. The next option comes off the double screen, also covered earlier in this chapter. 4 can cut high or low, but our defender goes hard over high. This is a multiple screen and is defensed as such. We have faced the Wheel many times, and we cannot remember this pass being completed or our defenders having to switch. The last option is the screen away from the ball by 3. The defense of that part play is also covered earlier in this chapter.

3. *The Shuffle:* Diagram 7-13 shows the options of this world famous pattern originated by Bruce Drake and perfected by Joel Eaves.

The first penetrating option is the pass from 2 to 3; and, as is mandatory by our basic principles, we contest this pass, trying to force the reception outside shooting range. 3 now can

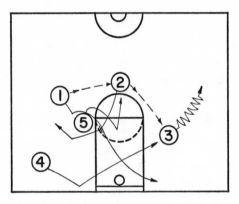

Diagram 7-13

work one-on-one on his defender, an isolation move. 1 then tries to rub his man off on 5. Earlier in this chapter we showed the coverage of the vertical and horizontal rub-off. The second option is the screen away from the ball, 2 setting the screen on 5, for a jump shot. Screens away from the ball have never been highly successful against our coverage, discussed earlier in this chapter. The third part play is an individual cut by 4, which we call the flash pivot cut, and we have covered the defense of this in Chapter 5.

4. *The Weave:* There are many ways to get into a weave: a three man weave, a four man weave, a five man weave, a weave with screens and rolls, a head-hunter weave. But, regardless of the method of entry, the result is a dribbling screen with an effort for a jump shot over the screen or a driving

lay-up. We have discussed defense of the dribbling screen earlier, and we apply it to destroy the weave. The continuous activity of the weave stresses openings by causing the defense to collide or get confused. We like the man guarding the passer to step back while the defender guarding the receiver is to step up. This gives us a perfect slide through, preventing confusion resulting from switching, and this technique prevents collisions.

5. *The 1-3-1:* Ray Mears's tremendous success with this highly disciplined game has encouraged the use of this offense in many high schools in our area. One of its basic patterns is shown in Diagram 7-14.

The pass from 1 to 2 is not really a penetrating pass so we allow it without contesting. Then comes the vertical rub-off by 1, defended earlier in this chapter. We now have 2, who can

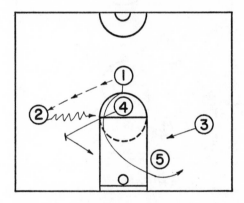

Diagram 7-14

go one-on-one if 4 clears, and 4 working a screen and roll. Not only is this a screen and roll maneuver (defensed earlier in this chapter) but we also have a wing and a center cooperating on the maneuver. We discussed the center hedging move in Chapter 5 which is perfect coverage of this offensive part pattern.

There is a lot of one-on-one or isolation action in this offense. A review of Chapter 1 would defense these moves properly.

6. *The Triple Post or Triangular Sideline Series:* With

Virginia Tech using this offense for four or five years, it was natural for many local high schools to adopt it. It is generally thought that Fred (Tex) Winter was the originator. And now that Roanoke College under Charlie Moir has won the NCAA College Division Championship using this attack, it will probably become more popular locally.

Diagram 7-15 shows the first half of the option. We try to contest the pass from 1 to 3, and we try even harder to eliminate a return pass in the corner. But 3 might get the ball into 5, and we play our normal pressure defense on 5 to prevent this (Chapter 5). Should the pass be received by 5, we play the split the post as described earlier in this chapter.

If 3 is unable to get the ball into 1 or 5, he passes back

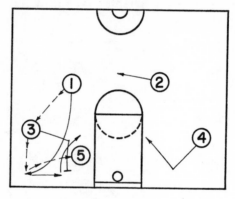

Diagram 7-15

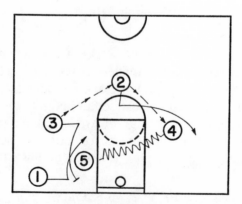

Diagram 7-16

around to 4 (Diagram 7-16). 2 and 4 then run the blast, which we defensed in this chapter. If this fails, 4 begins a dribbling screen toward 1, which we defensed also in this chapter and above as it might develop into a weave.

SUMMARY

We only presented the most famous patterns of these offensive series, and then we showed how we break them into part plays and defense them. These series have many more patterns with many more options and skilled operators to run them. This complicates the defensive game planning. But a mastery of scouting and the methods of defensing part plays will provide the defensive team with a fundamental defense to harass even the most famous offenses.

It provides the defenders with an opportunity to grow basketball wise and to play vicariously for one of those famous coaches.

EIGHT

Team Defensive Plays, Patterns, and Strategy

Coaches have devised offenses to exploit the defenses. Why not defensive patterns to nullify the offenses? We have them, and we call these patterns stunts.

This chapter deals with many of our favorite stunts. Of course, the imaginative coach can dream up many of his own. We would ask only that he invent these stunts in a scientific manner, using the gym as his laboratory.

We operate primarily from man-to-man pressure, and we full court zone press a great deal. We do this in a variety of ways, and we think our fundamental approach and its year-to-year carry-over value enables us to build this mountain of defensive stunts in a relatively short practice time.

HOW TO READ THE OFFENSE

For best defensive effort each defender must be able to recognize what the opposition is trying to do. The first time the opposition runs a pattern they might be successful. The second time only moderate success should be achieved. By the third running, if the defense can read offenses at all, the pattern should be thoroughly stopped.

Each coach has witnessed a team whose offense is growing ever weaker as the game progresses. What has happened is the defense has begun to read the offensive play patterns, and the defense has completely adjusted.

The coach can help his team discover the patterns the opponents will run. We scout our opposition thoroughly. Then we have all members of our team run our opposition's attack. We post this attack around our team room until our game with that opponent is over.

Each time the defenders run the opponents' patterns they learn how to recognize a new offensive play. Each year they retain and add to their repertoire. That is one reason why experience is so valuable.

We borrow movies to try to teach our team to recognize offensive patterns. Many colleges are happy to loan high schools some of their films. We require our athletes to diagram the plays used by one team or the other. Then we have the players analyze into part plays each of these patterns. The coach will be surprised how quickly the better defensive players will recognize patterns. And how quickly they can diagram them, defense them.

We like to take our returning squad to an all-star game during the summer. We require diagramming of the patterns run; or as most all-star games degenerate into individual movement, we require recognition of individual cuts. A few years ago we attended the Tennessee All-Star game, and our kids recognized the patterns immediately and began calling out the names we had assigned to the basic patterns being run. Of course the east squad ran some patterns that were nationally famous; however, it was refreshingly pleasurable to note that our teaching was not in vain.

During the off-season we open our personal library to our players. We like them to read the patterns of many of the published coaches. We also have the players break these patterns into part plays.

Television offers a great opportunity. The players can be asked to diagram plays of one of the colleges that is playing.

We live in an area where there are many college games tele-vised. And on Sundays the professionals play.

THE LONG ARM PLAYER AND WHAT TO DO WITH HIM

The long arm player is most valuable to a pressure defen-sive ball club. Most ball clubs have one; he is often untrained. He is a thief extraordinary, so we call him the long-arm bandit. If he is big enough, the best position for him is in the center of the court. He can be taught to create false security in the minds of his opponents. The player possessing the ball will toss passes to the bandit's man, thinking him to be in the clear, only to see the long arms of the bandit deflecting the pass. In our experiences with such players, we have found that other teams cannot adjust because of the mental or optical illusion-ary deception.

THE QUICK PLAYER AND HIS STRATEGY

We define the quick player as the player who is quicker than the man he is guarding. At any one time a team could have a minimum of none and a maximum of five. We use these quick players as the interceptors on our zone presses. On our man-to-man presses, he overplays any pass into his man from out of bounds. He can keep his man from getting the ball because he is quicker. This usually leaves him in a position as interceptor on our man-to-man press.

As interceptor, he has the best chance to use his quick-ness to our advantage: stealing the pass. Also, should he miss the interception, the quick player should be able to recover sufficiently to avoid the lay-up.

We like to have our quicker players in the spearhead attack of our three man press. We also use a four man and a caller press. We use the quick player as the caller in this press.

In our half court stunting defenses, we use the quick player to shoot the gaps. If one of our forwards is the quick player, we double-team with two guards and let that forward shoot the gap, an excellent stunt. If the quick player is a guard, we double-team with a guard and a forward, shooting the gap with the quicker guard. Our coaches usually decide which of our players are going to be quicker than our opponents. We then decide the quickest of these quick players. The quickest is designated the quick player for that game.

The quick player should sink inside whenever his man does not have the ball. He is then in position to help, and he is quick enough to recover on his man should a return pass be thrown.

HOW TO STOP THE SUPER STAR

Books can be written on how to stop the super star. There are that many different ways. We have played against many who have gone on to stardom in large and small colleges. We have used many different defensive strategies in stopping these stars.

Although strategy may differ from one star to another, we usually like to try to keep them from getting the ball. And if they go exclusively to the star, we double-team when he does get the ball. If he is a better passer than shooter, we usually will prevent him from driving. If he is a big man and plays inside, we usually run a pressure zone, using pressure tactics on the ball and sinking on the super star.

A super star who does not play team ball will not beat a team often. We do not advocate use of any of the Chinese Defenses: box and chaser for example. We like to play them straight, matching them up with the one man on our team who can exploit their weakness: greater height versus smaller men, quicker players on the slower star, letting the star shoot from the outside holding down the rest of the team, etc.

We do not like to weaken our team either physically or mentally by using trumped up defenses. Although we have on occassions trumped up defenses to halt the super star, it is not usually necessary. And on many occassions, the strategy will backfire.

In general, a coach should make use of his defensive strengths, nullify his weaknesses, exploit the opposition weaknesses, and nullify their strengths. As strengths and weaknesses change, the strategy will change.

INDIVIDUAL STRATEGY FOR THE GOOD OF THE TEAM

Each coach should know his individual players well. He

should know their quickness, their speed, their aggressive-
ness, their jumping ability, their desire: everything that is possible to know. Then, when assignment time comes, the coach
should assign his individual players in the manner that will
best aid his team. This changes from game to game.

After each game, we give our players mimeographed
paper which asked about their opposition player's (the man
they guarded) strengths and weaknesses. We file these; they
are accumulative. Along with the coaches' scouting reports,
they form a comprehensive file. This enables us to deploy our
individuals in the manner best suited for team results.

FORCE BACKDOOR, THEN SHOOT GAP

This is one of our favorite and most used stunts. It is most
effective against the two guards-three men under offensive
attack.

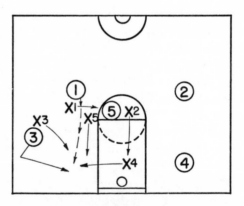

Diagram 8-1

We purposely overplay our corner men; or, if a point
offense the wing men force the offense backdoor. Diagram 8-1
shows the offensive guard, 1, seeing the forward, 3, open. He
immediately passes to 3; but X4, who has sagged to the area of
the bucket, as he is required to do on the weakside under our
defense, anticipates the pass and goes for the interception. X2
would rotate down to pick up 4; X1 would rotate over to 2, and
X3 would rotate out to pick up 1. This a typical move of the

1-3-1 zone defense. Sometimes we switch from man-to-man into 1-3-1 zone using this stunt.

This is not really a dangerous defensive stunt because, even if we fail to intercept, we still have zone or man coverage, whichever we desire. We also have X5, our big man, in perfect help position. X3 can help on 5 if 3 receives the ball and X5 has shifted to 3.

We usually call this maneuver while we are on offense; for example, our guard may say "one" while dribbling. Each player responds with "one." Now our opponents think we have called an offensive play while we have really called a defensive stunt. We also use this stunt over the full court, and it can result in interceptions, strengthening the full court man-to-man press.

DOUBLE-TEAM FIRST PASS ON PATTERN TEAMS

We love to play against the smooth-working, robot-like, pattern teams. They usually are slaves to their patterns, alternating from them only with other pre-planned options. A good scouting report will tell the defense where the options are after each pass. We combat this style of play by double-teaming the first pass and covering the pre-planned optional passing lanes. All we have to do is cover the lanes for five seconds, and we have a jump ball. If they try to force the ball into the options, we intercept. Strategically timed and sparingly used, this stunt can destroy the perfected rhythm of patterned teams. Do not use it two times in succession and do not use it more than two or three times a quarter, or the stunt will lose its effectiveness. Used successfully twice a quarter, it gives a net potential result of forty-eight points (the mathematical principle of basketball).

GIVE THE OUTSIDE, THEN TAKE IT AWAY

Sometimes at the half-court level but mostly with our full court defense, we like to give our opposition the outside lane, then take it away. It is an easy but highly effective stunt. We stay a few feet in front of the ball and a few feet to the inside. This creates the illusion of an open outside lane. When the offense has advanced the ball to a point most advantageous to the defense, we race in front of the dribbler, forcing the ball handler to change his direction, preferably on a reverse move. The double-teamer, upon seeing the beginning of the stunt, comes hard to set the double-team. The interceptors begin to fill the passing lanes. Its purpose is to create a perfect spot for a double-team, a spot that the offense cannot anticipate as it will change from possession to possession. Drill No. 67 is used to teach these techniques.

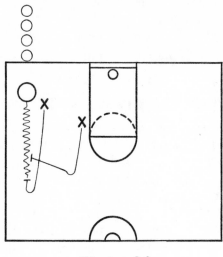

Diagram 8-2

Drill No. 67

Procedure

1. Line players up as shown; rotate from offense to defense to double-teamer to end of the line.
2. The defensive man covers the dribbler about two feet in front and toward the center of the court.
3. The double-teamer stays ahead of the ball as it is advanced down floor.
4. When the defensive man wants to cut off the dribbler, he does so.
5. When the dribbler is cut off, the double-teamer races over to double-team with the defensive man.

Objectives

1. To teach the defender how to give the outside then take it away.
2. To teach the defender how to force the dribbler to run the dribbling reverse.
3. To teach the proper approach and double-team stance.
4. To teach good offensive dribbling.

After mastering the techniques of double-teaming a reverse, giving the outside then taking it away, double-teaming in general, and shooting the gaps to fill the passing lanes, we are ready to begin our full court man-to-man defenses.

THREE RUN AND JUMP STUNTS

Before we teach the five-on-five stunt, we build our full court defense by a two-on-two, a three-on-three, and a three-on-two stunt. The two-on-two stunt is developed by the two guards pressing the two men bringing the ball up the court (Drill No. 68). The defender away from the dribbler races toward the dribbler while the dribbler's original guard races over to cover the vacated attacker. The three-on-three stunt (Drill No. 69) involves the same original move but a different rotation: as the defender away from the dribbling guard races toward the dribbler, the defensive forward comes up to cover the open offensive guard and the dribbler's original defender rotates to the vacated attacking forward. The three-on-two stunt (Drill No. 70) is used to stop two exceptionally talented ball handlers from advancing the ball. Using these stunts, any bad pass can be picked off and any completed pass can still be covered man-to-man.

Drill No. 68: Two Man Run and Jump

Procedure

1. Line players up in two lines (Diagram 8-3). The offense advances the ball down court and back, then we rotate from offense to defense to the end of the line.
2. 1 dribbles but X1 will not let him outside. 2 may

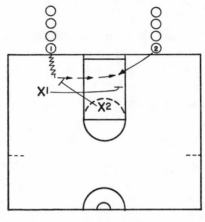

Diagram 8-3

never get above 1. X2 may never get below the line
of advancement of the ball.

3. When X2 wants, he runs directly at 1 as X1 forces
    inside. If 1 continues his dribble, he must charge X2
    or veer outside. If he veers outside, X1 continues his
    pressure and X2 helps. If 1 picks up the ball to pass
    to 2, X2 tries to deflect it as X1 races to cover 2 and
    we continue this run and jump the length of the court
    and back. If X1 and X2 steal the ball, they fast
    break. X1 and X2 hold their double-team as long as
    1 continues his dribble. If 1 and 2 cross, X1 and X2
    switch, creating the impression of a zone press.

Objectives

1. To teach the defenders how to play run and jump
    defense.
2. To condition the athlete for pressure defense and fast
    break offense.
3. To improve offensive ball handling.

Drill No. 69: Three Man Run and Jump

Procedure

1. Line players up in three lines (Diagram 8-4). The
    offense advances the ball downcourt and back, then

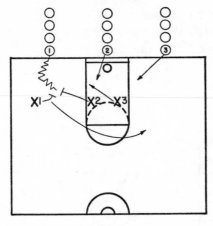

Diagram 8-4

we rotate from offense to defense to end of the line.

2. If 2, the center player, is dribbling, he must be going toward either 1 or 3. And in either case that is a two man run and jump (Drill No. 68). However, if either 1 or 3 is dribbling we force him to the inside and run our three man run and jump.

3. For discussion let's let 1 drive to the inside and run our three man run and jump. As 1 drives inside, X2 races toward 1 and double teams with X1 until 1 puts both hands on the ball. This is X1's cue to race hard to cover 3. Meanwhile X3 has shot the gap between 1 and 2 for the interception. Even if the pass is completed, we are still in a man-to-man press: X1 on 3, X2 on 1, and X3 on 2. And if the offense should turn the ball over the defense can fast break. The coach should require that the two offensive men without the ball stay behind the advancement of the ball. That not only expedites teaching but it permits more run and jumping per possession. And time is of utmost importance in the life of a coach.

Objectives

1. To teach three defensive men how to coordinate their efforts in a three man run and jump.
2. To improve offensive ball handling.

3. To teach proper methods of double-teaming.
4. To teach shooting the gap.
5. To condition the defensive players for full court pressure.

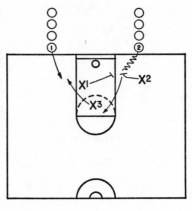

Diagram 8-5

Drill No. 70: Three Defenders Versus Two Attackers

Procedure

1. Line players up in two lines (Diagram 8-5). The offense advances the ball downcourt and back. X3 starts at safety on the way downcourt and X1 starts at safety on the way back. X2 is the first safety when the two lines rotate after a trip down floor and back.
2. X1 and X2 run and jump while X3 shoots the gap. After X1 and X2 stop 2's dribble, X2 drops and becomes the new short safety, waiting to shoot the gap on the next run and jump.

Objectives

1. To teach three defenders how to run and jump against two attackers.
2. To condition defensively for full court defense.
3. To teach double-teaming and shooting the gap.
4. To improve offensively the ball handlers.

FIVE MAN RUN AND JUMP

The three stunts above, along with the five-on-five described below, may be run regardless of the offensive move used. It is important that the entire defense be set ahead of the ball. And it is equally important that the defenders allow the dribbler a few steps in a definite direction before running at him.

When running the five-on-five stunt, the defender on the ball allows the dribbler to choose his direction. A defender who is stationed on that side of the court immediately runs directly toward the dribbler with his hands up and waving. The defender, who is running, must go directly toward the dribbler, head to head, as fast as he can without losing his body balance. Upon seeing this move, the other two defenders, not including the center or the two involved with the dribbler, rotate one man in the direction the ball is being advanced. The defender who initially had the dribbler drops to cover the first man in the opposite direction from the advance of the ball. Should the dribbler decide to reverse his direction, we do not drop his defender. We may double-team with him, or we may drop the defender who is running back to his original man. Usually the dribbler will not reverse but will pick up the ball and make a quick, easily intercepted pass. The defensive center covers the offensive center and zones it near the basket. If the defensive center is blessed with quickness, he may be included in the rotation.

In this stunt each offensive man is covered by one defender. The only moment anyone is open is at the instant of the double-team. And then the only open offensive man is the one immediately opposite the direction of the ball. That is the area where it is most difficult for the dribbler to make a successful pass.

If the stunt works, the defense has the ball; if it does not work, the defense still has each attacker covered man-to-man. And the new dribbler can be run at, starting the stunt again. It is as safe a stunt as a stunt can be. Its continuous running during each possession pressures and confuses the attackers to such an extent that they cannot set their offense in motion, nor can they handle the ball for long without a turnover.

THE ADJUSTABLE AREA MAN-TO-MAN PRESS

The adjustable area man-to-man defense described below is unique because the offense calls it by one of their basic maneuvers. The press is man-to-man unless the offense isolates to allow their best dribbler to attack it, then it becomes a zone press. The zone press would be either a 2-2-1 or a 3-1-1 depending upon the original back court alignment of the attackers.

To be successful against a zone press, teams cannot clearout: they must keep two or three attackers downcourt to advance the ball. But to have the most success against a man-to-man press, the offense must isolate, leaving one dribbler to advance the ball against one defender. Although this is primarily a man-to-man press that will not permit the isolation move, we begin by assigning our men zone areas, as in the 2-2-1 press (Diagram 8-23). From this 2-2-1 zone position, we initiate our press with X1 covering the first man on the left side of the court and X2 guarding the man who threw the ball in-bounds. Should the ball be thrown in on the right side of the court, X2 would get the receiver while X1 would get the out-of-bounds passer. If there is a third man in back court, the forward opposite the throw-in receiver would pick up this third man and X1 and X2 would still operate under the above rule. In the latter case the defensive forward on the side of the throw-in would become the short safety of the 3-1-1 zone press.

Once the ball is passed in-bounds, it is up to the offense to tell us which press to run. Should the attackers start clearing out, we immediately run either the 2-2-1 or 3-1-1 zone press with a quick double-team on the in-bound receiver (the zone press rotations will be discussed at the end of this chapter). If the offense keeps two or more men down floor to help bring the ball up court, we stay in a man-to-man run and jump, activating Drill Number 68, 69, or 70, whichever is applicable.

If the defense is to be a zone press, the front four rotate and concentrate on pressing while the deep safety, X5, concentrates on stealing errant, long, lob passes. The front four's rotation can create the illusion of being a man-to-man press.

Couple this with the rotation on a cutter and the defense can be quite confusing to even the most sophisticated of attacks.

The rotation on a give and go cutter is shown in Diagram 8-6. X2 covers the ball handler, 2, while 1 tries a give and go cut. X1, who had sagged toward the ball, goes with 1, preventing a return pass which would break the press. X3 would rotate to the area vacated by X1, and X1 would cover the area left open by X3. If it were a clearout by 1 for 2, X3 and X2 would double-team the ball. If 2 began dribbling X3 would run at him, activating the three man run and jump between X1, X2, and X3. X4 would prevent any penetrating downcourt pass.

If 1 runs a backdoor cut, breaks far behind X1, then X1 would release him to X3 and return to his original area, ready to run and jump, or zone press whichever is applicable.

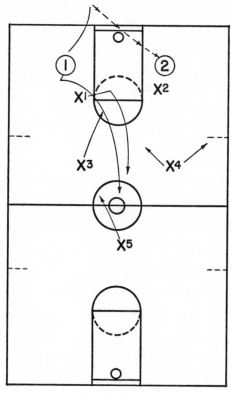

Diagram 8-6

A coach could activate Drill No. 70 during a game to prevent teams from attacking with two offensive men. The defense can easily bring down a forward, the one opposite the throw-in receiver, and run a three man run and jump versus two attackers with a two man tandem on their defensive end of the floor.

To alternate the effective use of this press, a coach could have X1 and X2 front the first two receivers to try to delay the in-bound pass (5 second violation) or to try to steal it. The in-bound passer cannot throw a lob over X1 and X2 without X3 or X4 intercepting. The defense could permit X3 or X4 to face guard the third potential receiver and have tight pressure on all potential receivers. Or if the offense chooses to attack with only two guards, X1 and X2 could double-team the single in-bound receiver. The defense could, if it were strategically beneficial, allow X1 to pressure the in-bound passer, bring up X3 as a wing defender, and create the impression of a 1-2-1-1 zone press.

The coach could also drop this defense to three-quarter or half court and be equally effective. The defensive team could run the two man run and jump or the three man run and jump anywhere on the court and at any time. The defenders could alter the amount of pressure applied on the ball handler; thereby either speeding up the game or slowing it down offensively.

FULL COURT MAN-TO-MAN PRESS

Constant pressure on both offense and defense is the cornerstone of our basketball philosophy. It naturally follows that we would use double-teaming pressures anytime the opportunity presents itself.

In order to double-team off man-to-man defense to its ultimate effect, all five men must be alert and act in concert as one. We have certain guidelines that help reduce the chance of error.

Unlike the pressure zones and zone presses, where each man's duty is expressly defined, the man-to-man stunts must be understood and recognized instantly by each man on the floor. We like to get this recognition by repeated drilling.

Drill No. 67 shows how we teach recognition of giving the outside, then taking it away. We progress this drill by placing another offensive man and another defensive man in the drill. When the double-team is set, the pass is thrown to the offensive man and the defensive man goes for the interception.

Drill No. 71 is used to teach recognition of a dribbling reverse. It is good to teach the teamwork necessary to good pressing teams.

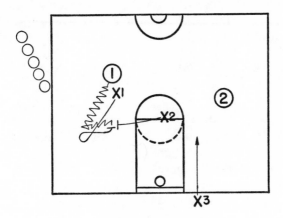

Diagram 8-7

Drill No. 71

Procedure

1. Line players up as shown; rotate from 1 to X1 to 2 to X2 (to X3 when he is in the drill) to the end of the line.
2. 1 goes one-on-one against X1. 1 tries to score.
3. X2 sags off his man our required step and a half toward the ball and is looking for the opportunity to double-team.
4. As long as 1 tries to score by facing X1, all X2 can do is sag and hedge, but should 1 run a dribbling reverse, turning his back to the defensive player, X2 immediately goes for the double-team.
5. We use this drill for both half court and full court recognition of the dribbling reverse.

6.   We progress the drill by adding X3 who is to shoot the gap on a pass from 1 to 2.

Objectives

1.   To teach 1 good one-on-one offensive moves and how to avoid the defensive double-team.
2.   To teach X1 to force 1 into a dribbling reverse.
3.   To teach X2 to recognize the dribbling reverse and then to apply our double-team mechanics.
4.   To teach teamwork on half court and full court double-teams.

Our next drill is a half court interception drill. When X1 and X2 set the double-team, 1 is instructed to pass to 2 (Diagram 8-7). X3 is now brought into the drill, and he is instructed to steal the pass. If the coach wishes to make it a full court drill, he can expand it by letting X3, the interceptor, keep dropping back downcourt as the ball is advanced up court. When the double-team is applied, X3 shoots the gap.

Our next progression is a continuation of the first two drills: we give X3 a man. We use this drill at half court and at the full court level. All three men are live, and as long as an offensive man on one side of the court has the ball, we instruct the double-team on reverses or in the corner. We also double-team if the ball and two men come together (screen and roll for example). This simply gives the offense two potential receivers, two men from which the defense must steal the pass.

Then we progress with all five men on the floor. The defense is to double-team under three conditions: in the four corners, on a dribbling reverse, or on any exchange where two men and the ball are involved. The defense is instructed to cover the passing lanes from the bucket out.

Diagram 8-8 shows a double-team in the corner. Diagram 8-9 shows a double-team out front. In both diagrams the logical pass is from 1 to 2; the logical interceptor is X3.

We usually try to double-team only off a dribble. Sometimes when teams lack imagination and adhere violently to patterns, we will double-team off the first penetrating pass. This has a tendency to make the offense move faster and throw off the timing of their smooth-pattern game.

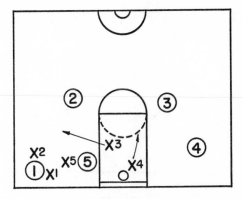

Diagram 8-8

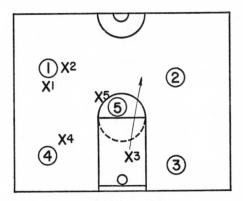

Diagram 8-9

We try to stunt over the full court in five ways: any reverse in the back court, any isolation by the offense, the first in-bound pass, as the offense crosses the midcourt line, and as two men and the ball come together.

We divide the full court into eight areas for teaching purposes (Diagram 8-10). We never double-team in the shaded areas. We never double-team with two high odd numbers or two high even numbers. In other words we will not send a man from region seven to double-team with a man from region five, nor will we send a man from region eight to double-team in region six. The reasoning is quite simple: this would allow our opposition an easy, uncovered shot from the corners

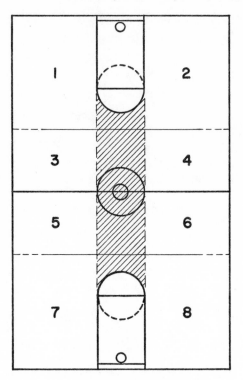

Diagram 8-10

within 15 feet. We also do not like two odd men or two even men to double-team, but we do allow this in backcourt pro-vided that there is no opposite of even or odd near.

By double-teaming with an odd and even man, we have better coverage of the down floor passing lanes. We can force the cross court pass to be a bounce pass if possible or a lob pass at least. The bounce pass is the slowest of all passes, the easiest to steal. The lob pass is next in difficulty of completion (see Chapter 6 for our method of forcing these passes).

There are three passing lanes: to the left, center and right. We cover the lanes with the lowest number on the ball side getting the ball side lane. The next lowest number gets the center lane. The lowest number off the ball side gets the cross court lane. The next lowest number off the ball side gets the center lane. If there is a defensive man in the shaded area, he would get the center lane. In other words the two smallest numbers get the outside lanes, and the largest number on one side gets the center lane. We call this our lane coverage rule.

Now let us look at four of the situations we described earlier (leaving out as two men and the ball come together) in the order that they might occur. The first is the in-bound pass. We start with man-to-man coverage, being alert to an in-bound pass. Again we try to force the bounce pass. Sometimes we run a facing press, four men and a caller, but mostly we just extend our sagging man-to-man to a full court length. The man-to-man coverage eliminates the advantage gained over a zone press by throwing the ball from one out of bounds position to another out of bounds position.

Diagram 8-11 illustrates a typical in-bound pass coverage. X1 shades his man inside. X2 covers his man tight, just like we cover the next receiver in a corner position. X3, X4,

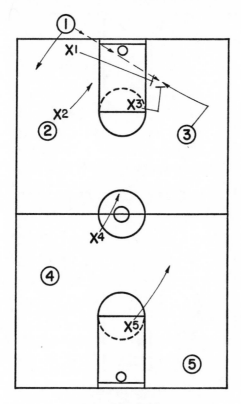

Diagram 8-11

and X5 sag toward the ball, keeping the ball and their man in their field of vision. Let us consider the most logical pass, in-bounds to 3. The in-bounds pass is one of the times we double-team while the offense still has the dribble. X3 must contain 3 until X1 can arrive with double-team help. X3 can accomplish this by creating an eight to ten foot cushion between himself and his man. X2 now has two men to cover, 1 and 2. X2 gets between them, ready to shoot the gap for the interception. Following our lane coverage rule, X4 would get the center lane, and X5 would get the ball side lane.

A lot of teams like to isolate against man-to-man presses. We are alert to this maneuver. Diagram 8-12 shows a typical move of isolation. As the reader can see by the moves, X3 and 3 are left in a one-on-one full court situation. Because of our

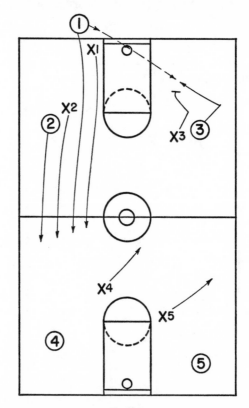

Diagram 8-12

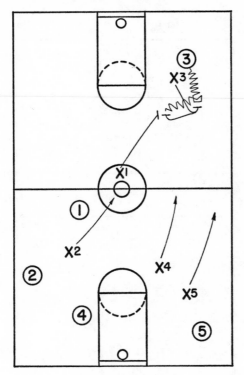

Diagram 8-13

double-teaming methods on in-bound passes, an isolation is obviously a dangerous offensive maneuver. However, for the sake of discussion, let us let them isolate. Diagram 8-13 pictures the position of the players when 3 starts his dribble downcourt. As in our half court double-teaming defense, X3 gives 3 the outside lane and then takes it away by forcing 3 to the middle by means of a defensive overplay. Our double-teamer waits to double-team until 3 runs a dribble reverse because this not only keys the defensive stunt but it gives us that extra fraction of a second to get our defense set. X3 and X1 do the double-teaming. X2 has the offside ball lane; X5 has the ball side lane and X4 covers the center lane.

Many teams never know when we are double-teaming the in-bounds pass and when we are going to let them isolate. They try to dribble the ball, yet leave men downcourt to help

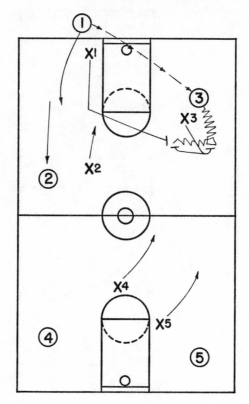

Diagram 8-14

out. We have a constant rule when pressing that we do not change: double-team all reverses in the back court. Diagram 8-14 serves as a good example. Again, the pass is in-bounded to 3, but the offense does not isolate, trying to protect against the quick double-team. 3 begins his dribble. We have a rule for all our full court presses: *No defensive man is allowed behind the advancement of the ball.* X1 is therefore even with or above 3 as he is dribbling. X3 is trying to force 3 into a double-team; X2, X4 and X5 have sagged toward the ball. X1 is waiting on 3 to reverse his direction by means of a dribbling reverse. When this happens, X1 and X3 will apply the double-team pressure. X2 splits his men, 1 and 2, looking for the quick pass back to 1. X2 is ready to shoot the gap. X4 is to take the center lane and X5 the ball side lane, according to our lane coverage rule.

The last of the strategic areas where we double-team is as

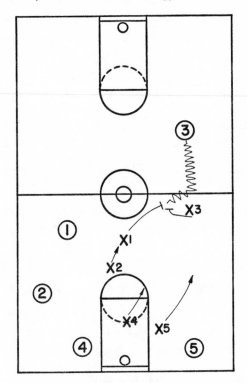

Diagram 8-15

the ball crosses midcourt. Diagram 8-15 shows X3 trying to force 3 into a double-team situation. X1 is to become the double-team helper. The other three have sagged, and they will cover the lanes according to our lane coverage rule.

As the reader can see, the defense is man-to-man until the double-team is applied. Then we cover the lanes in much the same manner as a zone press. The reader can also see that we have certain set rules which enable all five men to anticipate when the double-team is to be set. This allows all members of the team to act in concert as one. It has a further advantage of forcing all team members to be mentally alert, an advantage that makes a championship team out of mediocre material.

THE THREE MAN PRESS

We use a three man press which is exactly what the name implies. In fact one of the progression drills that we use to teach our full court presses, as previously mentioned, is three against three. We simply activate this drill in a ball game. It does not require as much gambling, and occassionally it results in a steal. But it serves to keep pressure on the ball, to keep a star guard from bringing the ball up court by double-teaming him, and to help us keep the opposition ever aware that we may press. The three man press can be used to control the tempo of the game. It is safe in that we have two big defenders left near the basket, and we can surprise a team that has become adapted to the three man press by activating the two big men.

We like to open the ball game with this press, double-teaming the good ball handler, forcing the ball to a weaker ball handler. Then we try to make this weaker ball handler commit an error, forcing him into a held ball or a bad pass.

FOUR MAN AND A CALLER PRESS

This press is used to keep our opposition from in-bounding the ball. The caller is our quickest man. He is stationed around midcourt watching the throw-in player. The other four men face guard the potential receivers. Whenever the ball is passed in-bounds, the caller heads in that direction, hollering the name of his teammate covering the intended receiver. The defender tries to deflect or intercept the in-bounded pass. If it is deflected, we expect the caller to retrieve it. If it is intercepted, we are on the fast break. If it is completed, the caller and the defender double-team while the other three race to the passing lanes. If the in-bounded pass is a lob pass, our quick caller should be able to at least draw the charge, or, failing at that, to contain the receiver.

We have never been hurt by using this press, and when using it sparingly, we have opened giagantic leads in otherwise close games. We call it from the bench.

THE ZONE PRESSES

The zone press should never be taught until the fundamentals of the man-to-man press are learned. We usually press the entire game with one or the other presses, and we like to use the zone press that best destroys our opposition's strengths. If we wish to apply instant pressure, we use the 1-2-2 zone press. If we wish to delay the opposition and intercept the long pass, we use the 2-2-1. We run our zone presses after a successful score or turnover near the baseline. We usually fall back into our half court man-to-man defense.

(1.) 1-2-2 Zone Press

X1 is our tallest forward. He is used as a double-teamer on in-bound passes. X2 and X3 must not let the pass be thrown over their heads. We let the ball be in-bounded in the corner area (shaded). X2 is our tallest guard. X3 is a tall, quick forward. X4, the interceptor, is our quickest man. We also like him to have long arms and be a good jumper. X5, the center, is our deep safety. If they put two offensive men at midcourt, we pull X5 up and play a 1-2-2 zone press.

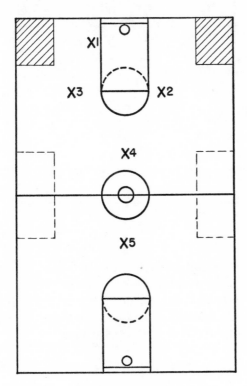

Diagram 8-16

The two areas where we like to double-team is shown by the shaded area and the broken lines.

If a pass comes into the right corner, X1 and X3 would double-team. X4 has the right passing lane, X2 the cross court passing lane, and X5 the center lane.

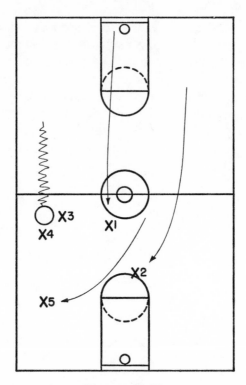

Diagram 8-17

If the opposition advances the ball past X2 or X3, it is X4's responsibility to halt the dribbler or pass receiver. Diagram 8-17 would then be our coverage as the ball goes down the right side beyond X3. X1 would have the cross court lane; X2 the middle and X5 the right side lane.

Drill No. 72

Procedure

1. Line players up as shown—be sure that all players

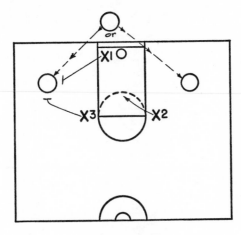

Diagram 8-18

trying for point and wing positions get drilled at those positions.

2. Out of bounds man throws pass into either receiver.
3. The two designated to double-team do that and the other wing man becomes the interceptor.
4. Sometimes we make this drill into a live three-on-three full court drill.

Objectives

1. To teach proper double-teaming.
2. To teach timing needed by the front three defenders on the 1-2-2 zone press.
3. To teach passing under pressure.
4. To develop conditioning, especially as the season progresses.

Drill No. 73

Procedure

1. Line players up as shown—be sure X1 and X4 are practiced by all potential point men and short safety men.
2. The man with the ball runs along baseline intending to throw to men at half court.
3. X1 follows the ball, keeping pressure on throwing arm of the passer. Most high school boys must point shoulder in direction of throw; they must put oppo-

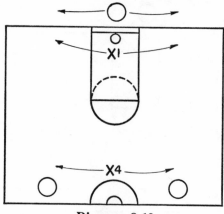

Diagram 8-19

site foot from throwing arm forward. X1 must force a lob pass.

4. X4 reads the feet and the eyes of the passer. X4 keeps readjusting his position (such as when ball is on right side, X4 shades to the right), intending to intercept pass.

Objectives

1. To teach baseball pass under pressure.
2. To teach point man to keep arms over shoulder of the passer.
3. To teach short safety to intercept lob passes.

Drill No. 74

Procedure

1. Line players up as shown—be sure to include the whole defensive team.
2. We let the dribbler advance ball until X4 has stopped him.
3. X3 then double-teams and the others cover their passing lanes.

Objectives

1. To teach complete team reactions as ball shifts positions.

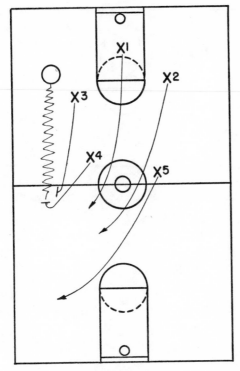

Diagram 8-20

2. To teach short safety to delay the drive until X3 can recover and double-team.
3. To teach proper defensive positioning by the rest of the team.
4. To teach offensive man to dribble without looking at ball.

Drill No. 75

Procedure

1. Line players up as shown—be sure that the personnel playing X1, X2, X3, X4 and X5 get to drill on their positions.
2. The double-team is set in corner by point and wing men.

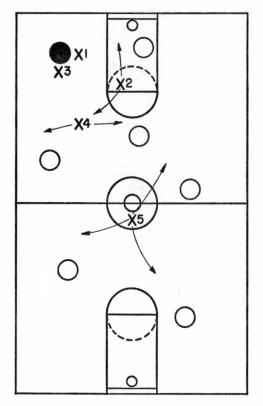

Diagram 8-21

3. The other defenders are set between two or more offensive men.
4. The offensive man with the ball may pass to either of the offensive receivers—the receivers may not move toward the ball to receive it.
5. The interceptors watch the legs and eyes of the passer in an attempt to steal the pass. The legs and eyes usually point in the direction of the pass.

Objectives

1. To teach double-team stance.
2. To teach the interceptor to be alert to his coverage lane.
3. To teach proper passing under defensive pressure.

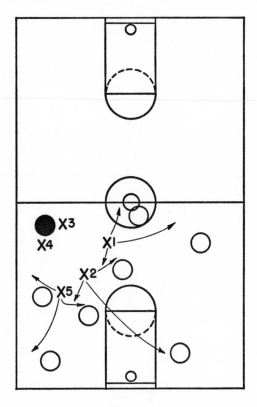

Diagram 8-22

Drill No. 76

Procedure

1. Keep players lined up as shown, making sure that each defender in the 1-2-2 press gets to play his position.
2. The double-team is set by a wing man and the short safety because ball has been advanced beyond mid-court.
3. The other defenders are set between two or three offensive men who cannot move to receive the ball.
4. The offensive man with the ball may pass to any of the receivers.
5. The interceptors are to study the passer and race to intercept the pass.

Objectives

1. To teach double-team stance.
2. To teach the interceptors to shoot the gap.
3. To teach proper passing under double-team pressure.

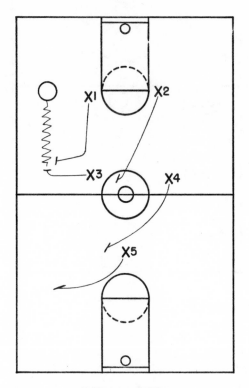

Diagram 8-23

(2.) 2-2-1 Zone Press

X1 and X2 are our guards; X3 and X4 are the forwards, and X5 is the center. We try to always keep the ball out of the center. We try to cover the downcourt men so that a long lob pass will be intercepted. We allow the offense to keep the ball in back court for ten seconds by permitting cross court passing.

If the ball is dribbled down the right side, we like to have the double-team set just before midcourt. That gives us another area of trapping from our zone and man-to-man presses. This keeps our opposition confused. X1 and X3 provide the double-team. X2 gets the cross court lane; X4 gets the center lane and X5 gets the strong side passing lane.

If an offensive guard chooses to dribble immediately inside after receiving the in-bounds pass, X1 and X2 would double-team. X3 and X4 would cover up court passing lanes while X5 would remain at safety.

We begin our drilling of full court presses by using the drills in Chapter 6. Then we move to Drills No. 68, 69, 70, 72, 73 and 74. We proceed from there into part drilling of the actual defenses by using Drills No. 75 and 76. A half taught full court press is detrimental to the defense; a thoroughly taught full court press can be disastrous to any offense.

TANDEM DEFENSE

Tandem defense is run by the first two defenders down court. In our three man press it would be the two big men. In our 1-2-2 zone press it would be the short and deep safety. In our 2-2-1 zone press it would be the deep safety and the weakside wing man. The personnel of the two-man tandem, therefore, varies from one defense to another so it must be learned by all defenders.

Its purpose is to prevent the lay-up. And if the defense can delay a shot a few seconds, all five defenders will have had time to retreat downcourt.

One defender yells "ball" and becomes the point man. The second defender immediately retreats to the basket and guards the baseline. The defender on the ball stays with the dribbler until a pass is made, then he retreats to the basket. The second defender immediately picks up the new pass receiver. If we can force two passes, the delay will have been sufficient to allow complete defensive recovery.·

We stunt out of the tandem. The baseline defender fakes going to his left, being sure that the dribbler sees him. Then, as the dribbler is prepared to pass to the defender's right, the dribbler's left, the baseline man shoots the gap for an interception.

SUMMARY

If the coach teaches the man-to-man press first, he can teach the zone press in a matter of minutes. Drilling on the press then builds the habits necessary to be successful.

As the reader noticed from our presses we spring them at different times, and we have them taught to provide the traps at different areas of the court. We try never to get beat downcourt as all men are required to stay in advance of the ball. That statement is the secret to good pressure defense: if a defensive team does not give the lay-up, it is not hurt by pressing the entire game.

Couple these presses with our half court man-to-man stunts, and any team will have a versatile, championship, pressure defense. But do not teach just the zone presses. They are only the clothes, not the true individual. The zones can be adjusted to by the great ball clubs, but the fundamental defense is difficult, if not impossible, to defeat.

NINE

The
Camouflage Zone

Although we are primarily a pressure man-to-man defensive team, we are cognizant that a good zone will defeat some teams that a man-to-man might not. We further believe that if the zone is camouflaged, it will have an opportunity to completely confuse the opponents. Nothing should be overlooked in a team's drive to win over all its opposition.

THE KEYS THAT CALL IT

We usually call our defense while on offense. We do not change many times during a game, just at strategic moments. A few years ago when our players were inexperienced we used one finger to denote 1-2-2 zone, two fingers to relate a 2-1-2 zone, and a fist to convey man-to-man. We used colors to signal the type of full court press we wanted to use: red for man-to-man, blue for 1-2-2 zone and white for 2-21 zone. We have played an entire game by switching full court presses after each score by our opponents; starting with red, alternating to white, then blue, and then repeating the sequence. We have in recent years let fruits represent one defense, meats another, and vegetables a third in our half court defense.

The reader can see that we try to train our players to

switch their defenses without using a time out. This forces our opposition into mistakes before the opposing coach can correct his team. We, the coaches, relay our defenses to our quarterbacks; we rarely, if ever, permit the players to call them.

THE STRATEGY FOR USING IT

We do not like to play straight zones for any duration. Such strategy would permit the opposition to set its offense with little or no pressure. Besides, today's guards, when left alone hit phenomenally from outside. But there are times when the defense is completely mismatched up front, when the opposition's patterns are working to perfection, or when the opponents have sprung an offensive surprise. It may be to the defense's advantage, under such conditions, to use a zone intermittingly.

We have also found that if we switch defenses a few times each quarter, it throws our opposition's game off. High school players do not easily adjust to changing defenses. When used sparingly, our camouflage zone has lasted off and on all night without being detected, resulting in many turnovers by our opposition.

In checking our DER charts we have found that good teams score in spurts: they score four or five times consecutively, then miss three or four times. We have found that if we switch to a camouflage zone the opposition does not continue their string. We used to have a set rule: call time out if the opposition scores three unanswered baskets. Now we do not waste our time outs there. Instead, we switch to our camouflage zone. It serves the same prupose as the time out: it cools the hot hand of our opposition.

THE ZONE DEFENSE, PRESSURE ZONES
AND PASSIVE ONES

Coaches in their preparations to defeat a zone teach the different zone defenses. They must have the zone defense taught so that their offenses can be practiced against them. Carrying that thinking a step further, it would be easy to teach all three basic zone defenses as part of a team's defensive structure.

We believe in all kinds of zones, the pressure and the

passive. It keeps basketball from becoming a stereotype game; it enables the thinker, the intellect to enjoy a sport. It puts added pressure on the coach and the players to react quickly in most pressure situations. It does not restrict strategy.

THE CAMOUFLAGE ZONE

The camouflage zone is exactly what the name indicates. It is a zone being used while the opposition think they are facing a man-to-man, or a man-to-man being used while the opposition think they are facing a zone.

Most man-to-man offenses, although they have extensive movement, are not designed to defeat zones. The one great offense that scores equally against both has not been invented. When we are confident that our team knows the man-to-man patterns our opposition is running, we may hide in our camouflage zone and play the passing lanes in an attempt to steal the passes. Most man-to-man offenses also utilize a lot of dribbling, and that dribbling is an advantage to the zone defense.

In our camouflage, we try to match up the offensive set of our opponents. If they have a point man with no high post, we are in a 1-2-2; if they have a two guard front, we are in a 2-1-2; and if they have a point man and a high post, we are in a 1-3-1. This leads our opposition to believe we are still in a man-to-man. And, as previously mentioned, we only camouflage a few times each quarter.

Sometimes our opposition recognize that we are in a zone, and they begin resetting into their zone offense. While they are doing this adjusting, a key word puts us back into a man-to-man defense. And there is not enough movement in the best of zone offenses to defeat even the weakest of man-to-man defenses. When we do use the key word to switch to man-to-man, we do not take an assigned man but the man in a defensive area.

(1.) 1-2-2 into 1-3-1

We make our conversions as simple as possible. Should we be in a 1-2-2 and wish to change into a 1-3-1, we move X5 high and let X4 cover baseline. X5 is our big center, and we want to keep him as near the middle as possible (Diagram 9-1).

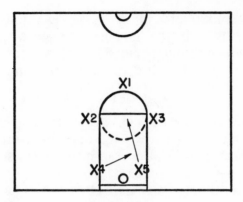

Diagram 9-1

(2.) 1-2-2 into 2-1-2

To switch from 1-2-2 into 2-1-2, X1 moves to the right, X2 steps up, X5 moves into the center and X3 moves to right forward (Diagram 9-2). This matches most offensive ball clubs really well because they would rather go down the right side, making our adjustments easier.

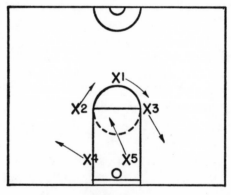

Diagram 9-2

(3.) Zone defense with man-to-man principles

We do not begin our original line-up in a 1-2-2. We begin in the line-up of the offensive set. But if the defensive team is taught to change from 1-2-2 to 1-3-1 to 2-1-2, they will be able to change in an associative order: that is from 1-3-1 to 1-2-2 to

2-1-2, etc. Usually few changes are required to stay in a zone yet appear to be in a man-to-man. This gives the defense a zone defense away from the ball and a man-to-man coverage on the ball.

We taught the match-up zone rules a few years back, and we found that it was effective. But the match-up zone should be used as a primary defense, and we have found that our man-to-man is a superior base from which we can teach our mountain of defenses. So for our purposes, the camouflage zone has been perfect. It gives us a change of pace when it is strategically advantageous for us.

(4.) Combining the odd and even zone

Some man-to-man offenses, such as the wheel, start with a two guard front and after one pass evolve into a one guard front. This makes it mandatory for us to be able to switch from two guards to one guard defensively. For discussion, we will let the offense go down the left side. X3 would have the forward with the ball (Diagram 9-3). X1 would have sunk,

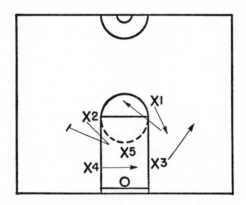

Diagram 9-3

looking like man-to-man, but still be ready to guard the new point man. X2 would be a new wing zone man and he would cover the weakside pass receiver as the ball would be swung back around. X5 and X4 would be covering the double low post. As the ball is passed back around (Diagram 9-4), X2 would cover the wing (regular 1-3-1 coverage), X4 covers

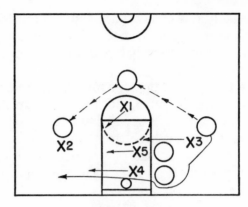

Diagram 9-4

baseline as in the 1-3-1 zone, X5 covers in a straight line with the basket and the ball (regular 1-3-1 zone defense), X1 sags to the middle as in man-to-man or 1-3-1 coverage, and X3 becomes the offside wing man. What we have done is change from a 2-1-2 zone into a 1-3-1 zone against a man-to-man pattern, the wheel.

Do not attempt these maneuvers, however simple they may appear, without ample practice. The defensive players will like them as a quick thinking change of pace. These maneuvers will confuse the opposition, and, remember, the defense is only a "word" away from man-to-man.

Be sure each opponent is scouted thoroughly. We are firm believers in knowing what our opposition intends to do. Without prior knowledge of what the opposition will do, it would be extremely difficult to camouflage the zone defensive stunts.

THE STRAIGHT 1-3-1 ZONE

There are those nights when a zone is just what the doctors order. We like the 1-3-1 because it goes along best with the rest of our defensive strategy. Each year at the beginning of practice we issue on a mimeographed sheet these rules for each position.

Point Man: the smallest guard

    1.   Meets the ball at midcourt.

2. Forces ball to one side—let the offense choose the side.
3. Responsible for blocking passing lane between the two outside guards—play halfway between these two men—stay within the confines of the lane extended downcourt.
4. If ball goes into corner, point man goes way down into lane to help keep ball out of post positions.

Weakside Wing: the other guard or the smallest forward (Weakside refers to side away from the ball)

1. Stay in a direct line with corner and ball; as ball goes into corner, the weakside man would go down.
2. If ball is deep in corner, he has at least one foot in the lane.
3. If lob pass is from one guard to the other, run at offense and force him outside (inside if the personnel is best suited to handle it).

Strong Side Wing: the smallest forward or other guard (Strong side refers to ball side)

1. Plays at least as high as foul line extended.
2. Closes passing lane to corner—force lob or bounce pass.
3. When ball goes into corner, wing man may:
   a. turn and face ball, or
   b. sink into foul lane and help on post coverage.
4. If ball gets inside, wing man sags, forcing ball out.
5. If overload on his side, he is to stay between the two deepest men.

Baseline Man: tallest forward or if defense has two real small guards, the tallest guard

1. Stays in line with ball, follows ball, protecting basket.
2. On flight of lob pass to corners, he rushes at offensive man, forcing him inside (outside if the personnel is best suited to handle it.)
3. If we have a tall baseline man, we try to block the shot.

4. If ball penetrates inside, baseline man goes directly to the basket and zones.
5. If he is screened, he has to fight through screen. If everyone else is forcing lob pass, he should be able to get to his man by the time he receives the ball.

Post Man: this is our tallest man, the center

1. Stays between ball and basket, making himself as big as possible.
2. If guards dribble into holes between zone men, the post man pressures high.
3. Should always front high post man unless he comes out as high as the circle.
4. Should have his hands in all penetrating passing lanes.
5. If ball is on side, post man should still front offensive pivot.

We have three drills that help us develop the timing needed for our 1-3-1 zone defense to be successful. The first drill is designed to teach the point man and baseline man their much needed cooperation. The next drill, No. 78, teaches the wing men their proper coverage, and Drill No. 79 combines the efforts of all four men.

Drill No. 77

Procedure

1. Line players up as shown—be sure each potential point and baseline man gets to work those positions.
2. No diagonal passes allowed—must pass ball around horn.
3. Only corner men can shoot.
4   X1 must make 1 and 2 lob ball if X4 is to have chance to cover both corners.
5. Players may not dribble or move.

Objectives

1. To teach offense to shoot as they receive the ball.
2. To teach lob passes.
3. To teach X1 and X4 how to cover their positions.

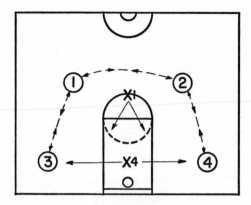

Diagram 9-5

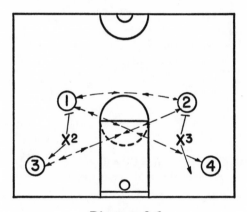

Diagram 9-6

Drill No. 78

Procedure

1. Line players up as shown. Be sure all potential wing men get to run these positions.
2. Passes must be made diagonal. 1 and 2 may throw semi-lob pass.
3. Only the guards, 1 and 2, may shoot. If 3 or 4 should receive a cross court pass, they may shoot lay-up.
4. X2 and X3 must learn their proper positioning; they must intercept cross court passes.
5. 1 and 2 may not dribble or move.

Objectives

1. To teach the guards to shoot quickly and accurately.
2. To teach cross court passing (not an offensive sin).
3. To teach proper defensive wing coverage.

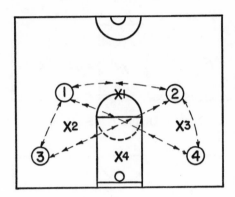

Diagram 9-7

Drill No. 79

Procedure

1. Line players up as shown. Be sure all potential wing men, pointmen, and baseline men get to work their positions.
2. All passes are permitted.
3. X1, X2, X3, and X4 must learn proper coverage of their position.
4. Offensive players may not dribble or move.

Objectives

1. To teach offense to attack a 1-3-1 zone.
2. To teach good, quick shooting.
3. To teach good, quick passing.
4. To teach proper defensive positioning for point men, wing men and baseline men.

It is rare indeed that we run a straight zone defense for any length of time, but it is always advisable to have a good one available. Games have been lost by stubborn coaches who refuse to run zone defenses.

THE 1-3-1 ZONE INTO MAN-TO-MAN

This is our camouflage working in reverse order. Our opposition knows us as a 1-3-1 zone team: that is, if we are not in man-to-man, we will be in a 1-3-1 zone. We may run the 1-3-1 for a few possessions, gravitating gradually into a man-to-man.

Most teams attack a 1-3-1 zone with a two guard front. To slip from 1-3-1 into man-to-man, the baseline defender, X4, must take the initial penetrating pass (Diagram 9-8). X4

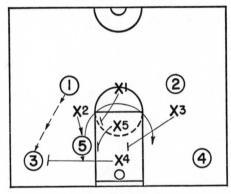

Diagram 9-8

has man coverage on 3. When the pass comes back around the horn, X2 would have 1, X1 would have 2, and X3 would cover 4. X5 would naturally cover the opposition center. This gives us a man-to-man coverage while our opposition think we are in a zone. It works a few times each quarter. We call it our "orange" defense. To further camouflage this stunt, we switch on all crossing of offensive personnel.

RETROSPECT

We do not like to scrimmage unless it is controlled. However, we will sometimes work on special strategy, like 3 points down and one minute left to play. Defensive poise is developed by use of the drills in this book.

We believe that any defense will be more effective if it has been drilled on until the moves are instinctive. Instinctive moves are quicker than moves by reaction, and quickness is of primary importance on defense. So a key to excellent defense is to drill, drill, drill until the movements are habitual.

We mix up our defenses, staying in our basic or primary defense mostly, but never letting our opponents get used to it. And, as the reader has undoubtedly noticed, we keep constant pressure on the ball, and we seal off the penetrating passing lanes. Pressure defense has given us our winning power.

Index